Jonas Feller

CSR Strategies in International Business

Concepts and theories for a competitive edge

Anchor Academic
Publishing

Feller, Jonas: CSR Strategies in International Business. Concepts and theories for a competitive edge, Hamburg, Anchor Academic Publishing 2016

Buch-ISBN: 978-3-95489-481-9
PDF-eBook-ISBN: 978-3-95489-451-2
Druck/Herstellung: Anchor Academic Publishing, Hamburg, 2016
Covermotiv: © pixabay.de

Bibliografische Information der Deutschen Nationalbibliothek:
Die Deutsche Nationalbibliothek verzeichnet diese Publikation in der Deutschen Nationalbibliografie; detaillierte bibliografische Daten sind im Internet über http://dnb.d-nb.de abrufbar.

Bibliographical Information of the German National Library:
The German National Library lists this publication in the German National Bibliography. Detailed bibliographic data can be found at: http://dnb.d-nb.de

© Anchor Academic Publishing, Imprint der Diplomica Verlag GmbH
Hermannstal 119k, 22119 Hamburg
http://www.diplomica-verlag.de, Hamburg 2016
Printed in Germany

Table of Contents

1 Introduction

For multinational enterprises (MNEs) to successfully gain and retain competitive advantages in an international environment it is vital to develop a clear strategy (Inkpen & Ramaswamy, 2006). Corporate social responsibility (CSR) becomes increasingly accepted as an important part of successful strategies (Galbreath, 2006; Husted & Allen, 2007; Husted, Allen, & Rivera, 2010; Porter & Kramer, 2002, 2006, 2011). While links between strategy and CSR can be traced back to the stakeholder model (Freeman, 1984), it is only recently that strategic CSR has been linked to the field of international business (IB).

This is partially because research on CSR has been largely confined to the developed world (Egri & Ralston, 2008; Muller & Kolk, 2009). Similarly, IB literature tended to neglect the field of business ethics (Doh, Husted, Matten, & Santoro, 2010). As a result, little is known about strategic CSR in an IB context (Arthaud-Day, 2005; Doh et al., 2010; Egri & Ralston, 2008; Rodriguez, Siegel, Hillman, & Eden, 2006). At the same time, it has been observed that "CSR is becoming a very important component in international business" (Yang & Rivers, 2009, p. 165).

Accordingly, this book attempts to answer the question of how MNEs manage CSR in a globalised world strategically. In particular five questions arise: Can CSR become standard-ised and managed by the head quarter? Can CSR become responsive to local demands when managed by the subsidiary? Is a combination of global and local CSR recommendable? What are the decisive variables that influence strategic decisions with regards to CSR? Does the concept of shared value offer a solution for the aforementioned questions?

A critical literature review is conducted, intending to provide a comprehensive summary of the answers offered. The study recognises current efforts for developing a unifying frame-work for the evolving concept of strategic international CSR (Hah & Freeman, 2014). It contributes by collecting theoretical frameworks and empirical studies examining the outlined questions. Hence a clearer image emerges of a subject that has been described as being "under-explored" (Yang & Rivers, 2009, p. 155), "embryonic" (Rodriguez et al., 2006, p. 733), "complex and unclear" (Garriga & Melé, 2004, p. 51), and "much more difficult than it appears" (Galbreath, 2006, p. 180). A concluding discussion aims to address both implica-tions for management and academics.

Scholars argue that connecting CSR, IB, and strategy yields benefits for companies as well as societies (Palazzo & Scherer, 2006; Porter & Kramer, 2006). As unambiguously indicated by the fast growing body of recently published articles on strategic CSR in IB, the need for connecting these fields of research has become widely accepted. With the financial, social, and ecological crises challenging business and society alike, this interest is not likely to diminish any time soon.

The remainder of this study is structured as follows. Chapter 2 deals with the methodology applied. Chapter 3 briefly introduces the foundations of CSR, IB and strategy. As it becomes clear as to how these subjects relate to each other, the major question of this study logically emerges: How do MNEs manage CSR in a globalised world strategically? Chapter 4 is about answering this question. The global and local CSR strategies are examined first. Antecedents and outcomes of the respective approaches will be discussed based on theoretical frameworks and empirical evidence offered by academic literature. As limitations of the opposing perspectives emerge, papers with a transnational approach are discussed followed by an examination of findings on variables that could influence CSR strategies, namely distance, industry and visibility. Finally, the concept of shared value is discussed.

We conclude with a critical summary of the literature reviewed. Chapter 5 accordingly compares emerging concepts, remaining contradictions, and conspicuous patterns. Managerial implications for strategy as well as limitations and resulting questions for future academic research complement this chapter. Last but not least, Chapter 6 briefly summarises the key findings.

2 Methodology

The present study intends to answer the outlined research questions on international strategic CSR by means of a critical literature review. This methodology is applied to present key findings on a subject with a view to combining different streams of research logically. In the present case of an emerging subject reviewing the literature may provide much needed clarity and a comprehensive overview of existing assumptions and findings. The critical examination of the literature available attempts to evaluate the different contributions, to explain conflicting findings and to suggest directions for future research (Saunders, Lewis, & Thornhill, 2009).

As indicated by the research questions, no prior expectations regarding the outcomes were made. This inductive approach towards the literature review is appropriate especially since the evolving subject of international strategic CSR still lacks consensus and a unifying framework (Hah & Freeman, 2014). The study accordingly attempts to collect, structure and analyse what has been provided by researchers.

The process of collecting the literature started with a clear definition of the scope of this paper, i.e. the connection of CSR, IB and strategy. In accordance with Fisher and Bonn (2007) the strategic perspective on CSR implies that purely normative approaches to CSR are found to be out of scope of this literature review. Subsequently, search terms were derived for the initial search. *CSR* and *corporate social responsibility* were combined with *international business, multinational enterprise, MNE, strategy, subsidiary, host country* and *shared value*, as well as combinations of the above. In a second step, key words provided by individual articles were added to the list of searched key words: *Global CSR, transnational strategy, institutional theory, global vs. local*, and *business ethics*. The searches were conducted by using the search engines *Web of Science* (WOS) and *CrossRef*. The services of these websites include searching a wide range of academic journals including the relevant business journals, particularly the *Journal of International Business Studies* (JIBS), the *Academy of Management Review*, and the *Journal of Business Ethics*. No restrictions regarding journals or the date of publication were made, ensuring a comprehensive body of literature to be included in the review.

During the process of examining the literature, additional searches were conducted so as to involve a variety of related papers. These provided a well-grounded understanding of theoretical concepts. The wide range of key words, the inclusion of referred articles and author-specific searches should provide for not overlooking important literature by considerably augmenting its body.

3 Evolution of concepts

Strategic international CSR builds on three distinct relationships: Business and society, business and globalisation, and business and strategy. A brief overview of each theme demonstrates the way in which they converged over time. Throughout the discussion it becomes clear why a comprehensive model is required to respond to this development.

3.1 Business and Society: Corporate social responsibility

No final consensus exists on the definition of corporate social responsibility (Freeman & Hasnaoui, 2011; McWilliams, Siegel, & Wright, 2006). CSR is a multi-dimensional concept (Lindgreen, Swaen, & Maon, 2009; Waldman et al., 2006) that "has remained vague and ambiguous" despite many attempts to define it (Schwartz & Carroll, 2003, p. 503). One definition refers to the lowest common denominator: "The foundation of CSR is the acknowledgement that businesses have responsibilities to society that go beyond shareholder wealth maximisation" (Font, Walmsley, Cogotti, McCombes, & Häusler, 2012, p. 1554). McWilliams and Siegel (2001) defined CSR as "actions that appear to further some social good, beyond the interests of the firm and that which is required by law" (p. 117). A broader, widely accepted definition by Carroll (1979) proposes that "the social responsibility of business encompasses the economic, legal, ethical, and discretionary expectations that society has of organizations at a given point in time" (Carroll, 1979, p. 500).

These diverging societal expectations can be linked to differences between cultures (Freeman & Hasnaoui, 2011; Waldman et al., 2006), the stage of economic development (Robertson, 2009; van Tulder & Kolk, 2001; Waldman et al., 2006), and the institutional environment (Doh & Guay, 2006; Lo, Egri, & Ralston, 2008; Matten & Moon, 2008). Another issue hampering a conclusive definition is "its interchangeable and overlapping character with other terminologies such as 'corporate citizenship', 'the ethical corporation', 'corporate governance', 'corporate sustainability', 'social responsible investment', and 'corporate accountability'." (Nasrullah & Rahim, 2014, p. 23). In some cases, these terms are explained as simply being synonyms of CSR (Kanji & Chopra, 2010). On the other hand, different scholars sometimes ascribe varying meanings to an individual term (Garriga & Melé, 2004). As a result, some authors maintain that the ambiguity and complexity associated with the concept does not allow for an exact definition (Matten & Moon, 2008; Palazzo & Scherer, 2006).

Instead it has been characterised as a "construct [that] describes the relationship between business and the larger society" (Snider, Hill, & Martin, 2003, p. 175).

Formal writings on CSR can be traced back to the middle of the 20th century. In 1953, Bowen published his book *Social Responsibilities of the Businessman*, marking the advent of the modern concept of CSR (Carroll, 1999). Bowen raised the initial question, which remains relevant until today: "What responsibilities to society may businessmen reasonably be expected to assume?" (Bowen, 1953, p. xi). A few years later, Davis (1960) introduced his *iron law of responsibility*, arguing that social power managers needs to be reflected by social responsibility. Failing to meet expectations of responsibility, Davis (1960) argued, would lead to a loss of social power.

This view was contested by Milton Friedman who famously warned that "the doctrine of 'social responsibility' involves the acceptance of the socialist view that political mechanisms, not market mechanisms, are the appropriate way to determine the allocation of scarce resources to alternative uses" (Friedman, 1970). Shareholder theory accordingly deems expenditure based on societal expectations as misuse of shareholders' funds (Garriga & Melé, 2004). The shareholder approach emphasises profitability over responsibility (Kolk & van Tulder, 2004).

Freeman challenged this "conventional view of the firm" whereby managers assume "exclusively fiduciary duties towards stockholders" (Garriga & Melé, 2004, p. 60). Instead, a variety of groups such as suppliers, employees and customers constitute parties that have a *stake* in the company. Since they are capable of influencing the company positively or negatively they fall within the scope of a managers' responsibilities (Freeman, 1984).

It has been argued that stakeholder theory is the antithesis to shareholder theory and that it emphasises responsibility over profitability (Bosch-Badia, Montllor-Serrats, & Tarrazon, 2013; Kolk & van Tulder, 2004). Hence, stakeholder theory is classified as a foremost ethical CSR theory (Garriga & Melé, 2004; Miska, Hilbe, & Mayer, 2014) in which "each group of stakeholders merits consideration for its own sake and not merely because of its ability to further the interests of some other group, such as the shareowners" (Donaldson & Preston, 1995, p. 67).

Throughout this paper, the emphasis on strategic CSR management implies that the descriptive aspect (what companies do) and the instrumental aspect (how companies attain their goals) is of interest whereas normative aspects (what companies ought to do) is outside the scope of this study (for a critique of this approach, see: Arnold & Valentin, 2013; Palazzo & Scherer, 2006; Schneider, 2014). This does not reduce the usefulness of stakeholder theory for strategic CSR. On the contrary, stakeholder theory "has emerged as the dominant paradigm in CSR" (McWilliams & Siegel, 2001, p. 118). Carroll (1991) noted there is a "natural fit" between CSR and stakeholders (p. 43). Stakeholder theory has been described as "the cornerstone of the business case for CSR" (Barnett, 2007, p. 796) since it provides a useful tool to identify groups towards whom business carries responsibilities, even if the long-term goal was to maximise wealth for shareholders (Sison, 2009). The diverging receptions of stakeholder theory reflect the fact that CSR theories generally focus on politics, economics, society and ethics (Garriga & Melé, 2004), depending on the scope of respective research and reasoning.

Furthering the understanding of CSR, Carroll (1991) suggests a pyramid of corporate social responsibility, encompassing four components. The basic component demands a business to *be profitable*. The legal responsibility, *obey the law*, is mandatory. The ethical responsibility, *be ethical*, encompasses the second duty in that society expects this behaviour, yet answering these expectations is not enforced by the authorities. Eventually philanthropic responsibilities require the company to *be a good corporate citizen* by donating and contributing to worthy causes.

While the pyramid represents a more detailed description of Carroll's (1979) definition of CSR which has been proposed earlier, it becomes clear that the fourth component is seemingly irreconcilable with Friedman's (1970) view. Carroll (1991) explicitly addressed this point arguing that a majority of companies embrace the notion of corporate citizenship and willingly donate towards a variety of issues.

In fact, as CSR is increasingly practised by corporations around the world (e.g., Kanji & Chopra, 2010; Peng & Pleggenkuhle-Miles, 2009), research has provided many reasons to embrace the concept. Evidence suggests that CSR activities may help gaining competitive advantages (Jones, 1995; Russo & Fouts, 1997), a favourable brand image (Lee, Oh, & Kim, 2013), mitigating risk (Husted, 2005), improving relationships with governments (Zhao, 2012) or avoiding stricter legislation (Campbell, 2007; Laudal, 2011; Waddock, 2008). Although much research has been concerned with possible positive correlation between CSR and financial returns (e.g., Margolis & Walsh, 2003; Orlitzky, Schmidt, & Rynes, 2003), Barnett (2007) concludes that even though not every CSR activity yields profits some do, with the overall relationship being positive. More recently, it has been shown that a positive trend between CSR and financial performance exists when specific aspects are measured and time is taken into consideration (Lu, Chau, Wang, & Pan, 2014).

Taken together, the CSR concept has continuously evolved during the past decades (for further readings, see: Carroll, 1999; Garriga & Melé, 2004; Werther & Chandler, 2006). Research offers multiple reasons for companies to embrace related activities. However, as these companies internationalise, they operate in distinct societies. This dramatically increases the complexity of their responsibilities. Carroll noted already in 2004 that the debate on CSR in the future moves towards global considerations, which leads to the field of international business.

3.2 Business and Globalisation: International business

Globalisation "can be defined as a process of intensification of cross-border social interactions due to declining costs of connecting distant locations through communication and the transfer of capital, goods, and people. This process leads to growing transnational interdependence of economic and social actors ..." (Scherer & Palazzo, 2011, p. 901). International business (IB) is closely linked to globalisation. It denotes the "performance of trade and investment activities by firms across national borders" (Cavusgil, Knight, & Riesenberger, 2012, p. 40). Probably the most prominent actor in IB is the multinational enterprise (MNE). This "is a large company with substantial resources that performs various business activities through a network of subsidiaries and affiliates located in multiple countries" (Cavusgil et al., 2012, p. 48).

The ongoing liberalisation of trade and the emergence of trading blocks spurred international business. The internationalisation of countless businesses was further driven by fundamental advances in technology which substantially reduced costs of communication and transportation (Cavusgil et al., 2012). MNEs naturally benefited from globalisation as one of their core functions involves operating across national borders. Greater flexibility allowed for restructuring every part of the value chain. Sales increased as new markets were entered, additional resources were tapped and production facilities relocated around the globe. Strange (1996) extensively covered this phenomena that changed the role and restricted the influence of territorial states. With power shifting towards world markets and large, multinational enterprises governmental institutions proved incapable of preserving most of their traditional problem solving capabilities.

Over time, the role of MNEs was questioned by society. Many if not most MNEs were accused of misusing their rising power. Numerous scandals shed light on issues ranging from fraud, bribery, exploitation, child labour and human rights violations to deliberate environmental degradation (Palazzo & Scherer, 2006). Multinationals were perceived to be the primary beneficiaries of increasing inequality, accused of giving implicit consent to endless human rights violations mainly in the third world (Giuliani & Macchi, 2014). In short, the international discussion of the merits and dangers of globalisation evolved largely around MNEs (Nason, 2008).

Much of the debate evolved around the increasingly unbalanced relationship between business, society and politics – especially in developing countries. As noted by Scherer and Palazzo (2011), substantial shares of the global value chain have been moved to locations with no rule of law and a lack of democratic institutions. In numerous cases laws exist or could easily be adjusted. However, as countries compete for investments, governments have been reluctant to enforce or improve their legislation, especially with regards to labour and environmental standards (Williams & Aguilera, 2008).

In such circumstances, already the second component of Carroll's (1991) pyramid – obey the law – becomes a challenging task. The component had been developed initially with the US environment in mind. The scholar accordingly revised the model, demanding from companies to "obey the law of host countries as well as international law" (Carroll, 2004, p. 118). At around the same time many publications started calling for and contributing towards a CSR concept that considers globalisation and international business (e.g., Arthaud-Day, 2005; Carroll, 2004; Logsdon & Wood, 2002; Meyer, 2004; Palazzo & Scherer, 2006; Snider et al., 2003).

This transformation was not limited to the theoretical realm. It has been recognised that MNEs carry a tremendous potential to contribute towards solving the pressing problems of the 21th century. Their capability to successfully operate in an international environment, vast knowledge and multiple resources are well designed to address poverty, environmental protection and scarcity of vital resources (Jamali, 2010; Kolk & van Tulder, 2010; Strange, 1996). In fact, Reimann, Ehrgott, Kaufmann, and Carter (2012) observed that MNEs increasingly pay attention to local problems. Sensitivity towards host country needs indicates a change that reflects awareness of the dangers associated with irresponsible behaviour. Scherer and Palazzo (2011) likewise admit that companies start assuming responsibilities that exceed legal provisions. This mitigates the problems caused by the absence of a global regulatory mechanism and creates new perspectives for both business and society alike.

It is interesting that this development was furthered by the internet. While initially being part of those technological advancements that facilitated the increase in international business, its social networks and blogs nowadays empower consumers and activists worldwide. For example, Lee et al. (2013) presented evidence from the conduct of the Fortune 500 companies indicating that irresponsible behaviour goes viral online, damaging the brand associated with it. On the other hand, responsible behaviour often brings about proactive consumer participation in social media. Without investing additional resources these companies' communication channels draw positive feedback and satisfied user comments. In a similar vein, Werther and Chandler (2006) argued that the recent wave of globalisation consists of two distinct phases. The first phase saw the unchallenged rise of MNEs, while the second phase witnesses empowered consumers and increasing international regulation.

Actually several initiatives were successfully launched to this end. Of these, the Global Compact framework initiated by the United Nations in 2000 has become the largest and most prominent (Nason, 2008). The network brings together more than 10,000 participants and encourages dialogue between companies and representatives of civil society (Voegtlin & Pless, 2014). It "asks companies to embrace, support and enact, within their sphere of influence, a set of core values in the areas of human rights, labour standards, the environment, and anti-corruption" (UN Global Compact Office, 2014). This has been supplemented by the Global Reporting Initiative (GRI) which provides guidelines for sustainable reporting, and the Principles of Responsible Investment (PRI) for private and institutional investors.

However much these efforts are important, any CSR policy presupposes the existence of a profitable enterprise. Carroll (2004) accordingly defined the first component of his global CSR pyramid as "do what is required by global capitalism" (p. 116). The most vital requirement concerns the careful consideration of strategic options – the foundation of successful competition in an international business context (Inkpen & Ramaswamy, 2006).

3.3 Business and Strategy: Integration and Responsiveness

Porter (1996) established that strategy is "essential to superior performance, which, after all, is the primary goal of any enterprise" (p. 61). It "is a planned set of actions that managers employ to make best use of the firm's resources and core competencies to gain competitive advantage" (Cavusgil et al., 2012, p. 345). A competitive advantage in IB refers to "organizational assets and competencies that are difficult for competitors to imitate and thus help firms enter and succeed in foreign markets" (Cavusgil et al., 2012, p. 179). This leads to the question of how to organise the assets and competencies of the MNE on a global scale.

Prahalad and Doz (1987), as well as Bartlett and Ghoshal (1998) identified two conflicting forces that have an impact on the decision: *Global integration* and *local responsiveness*.

Global integration emphasises "world-wide efficiency, synergy, and cross-fertilization" (Cavusgil et al., 2012, p. 350). Four key drivers for a global strategy can be distinguished: Market drivers (converging customer demands), cost drivers (economies of scale), governmental drivers (liberalisation) and competitive drivers (facing global competitors) (Morschett, Schramm-Klein, & Zentes, 2009). The organisation responding to these pressures will tend to integrate and centralise its activities.

On the other hand, local responsiveness considers the prevailing and strong differences between countries. Key aspects include different customer demands (e.g., due to standards of living, culture, climate), diverging legislation and also different competitive contexts (Morschett et al., 2009). The organisation adopting this strategy will decentralise much of its operations.

The integration-responsiveness (IR) framework builds on these conflicting implications. Bartlett and Ghoshal (1998) proposed an organisational typology which has found empirical support by Harzing (2000). The three types of organisational strategy are defined as *global* (high integration, low responsiveness), *local* or *multidomestic* (low integration, high responsiveness) and *transnational* (combining high integration with high responsiveness) (Harzing, 2000). Originally, a fourth type termed *local* or *multinational* was included describing a MNE that faced low pressure for both integration and responsiveness. Harzing (2000) found no evidence for this type of MNE and the present study accordingly does not further investigate this approach. The approach has been criticised by many scholars including Arthaud-Day (2005) as well as Husted and Allen (2006).

From the three remaining strategies the most sophisticated configuration is the transnational one. It aims to balance the need for efficiency (global) and flexibility (local). This is achieved mainly by a network structure where particular operations and resources will be assigned to individual subsidiaries. A successful implementation leads to economies of scale without a loss of flexibility for the MNE (Morschett et al., 2009).

Regarding both, strategy is essential for competitive advantage, which in turn is vital to a company's success. As mentioned earlier, CSR carries the potential to provide a company with competitive advantages. Porter and Kramer (2002, 2006, 2011) have convincingly concluded that this advantage is most likely to be achieved if CSR is managed strategically: "A company must integrate a social perspective into the core frameworks it already uses to understand competition and guide its business strategy" (2006, p. 84). This corresponds with Freeman (1984) who viewed his stakeholder model as a "concept [that] can be built into the strategic management process that exists in most organizations" (p. 83), and Galbreath (2006) who argued that CSR constitutes a strategic issue that ought to be part of the MNEs overall strategy. Oikonomou, Brooks and Pavelin (2014) present empirical evidence, indicating that MNEs that treat CSR strategically financially outperform competitors with no CSR activities, who in turn outperform MNEs that treat CSR in an inconsistent manner.

4 Strategic international social responsibility

The need for research on international strategic CSR is widely recognised (e.g., Arthaud-Day, 2005; Doh et al., 2010; Husted & Allen, 2006; Rodriguez et al., 2006; Yang & Rivers, 2009). This converges with increasing interest in and practice of CSR by MNEs (e.g., Porter & Kramer, 2011; Reimann et al., 2012). Accordingly, the following question arises: How do MNEs manage CSR in a globalised world strategically?

The organisational strategy developed by Bartlett and Ghoshal (1998) suggested that a global, local and transnational solution exists. This approach is promising since strategic CSR is also subject to pressures for global integration and local responsiveness (Bondy & Starkey, 2014). The integration-responsiveness framework was first explicitly linked to international CSR by Logsdon and Wood (2002, 2005). Supporting this approach, Arthaud-Day (2005) suspected clear implications of the organisational strategy on a companies approach towards CSR.

So far the strategic implications remain difficult to asses (Peng & Pleggenkuhle-Miles, 2009; Rodriguez et al., 2006). Scholars agree on a relationship between the product-market a company is catering for and its organisational strategy (Morschett et al., 2009). For example, highly standardised products need little adaptation to local customers and will thus be offered by a MNE with a global strategy (Harzing, 2000). However, regarding CSR this kind of clarity remains missing, which makes it "a particularly complex issue" for MNEs (Polonsky & Jevons, 2009, p. 330). Subsequently, the case for a global, local and transnational solution will be discussed separately. As their respective limitations become clear, possible impacting variables will be added. Finally the shared value concept is discussed with emphasis on a developing country context.

4.1 Global CSR

For Carroll (2004) CSR is ultimately moving towards universal norms that would necessitate a global approach to CSR. Ethical standards should be reconciled between the different locations of a company, moving towards global and universal ethics. This is in line with the Global Compact framework which draws on "a set of core values" (UN Global Compact Office, 2014) that should form the foundation of responsible corporate conduct. The global approach implies "a top-down, consistent set of policies and procedures to be implemented in all the company's local faculties" (Logsdon & Wood, 2005, p. 839).

The global approach builds on *certified standards* and *global leadership* with the strategic aim to become *globally consistent* and *efficient*. Although being interdependent, these four advantages require a separate examination. Certification refers to self-regulatory initiatives and standards that apply globally. Certificate issuing institutions require a company to apply the same standards throughout their different subsidiaries. Global leadership refers to a need for a unified approach towards CSR management. Findings indicate that national culture influences the perception and commitment to aspects of CSR. The global approach ensures a unified commitment across different cultures. Consistency is closely linked to branding and risk management. A consequence of consistency is upward harmonisation. Eventually efficiency is ensured by the centralised and standardised process of determining and implementing CSR.

4.1.1 Certified standards

Emerging global standards constitute the most important argument in favour of global CSR. In this case the head quarter is going to develop its CSR strategy based on these worldwide accepted standards, guidelines and norms. The substantial rise in certified standards indicates that MNEs as well as consumers and other stakeholders value and embrace this approach.

Emerging global standards include the "U.N. Universal Declaration of Human Rights, the OECD Guidelines for Multinational Enterprises, the Global Sullivan Principles of Social Responsibility, the U.N. Global Compact ..." (Logsdon & Wood, 2005, p. 59). In addition, the International Organization for Standardization (ISO) developed an international CSR standard, ISO 26000 (Waddock, 2008). This standard is supplemented by the ISO 14000, ISO 14031 and SA 8000, benchmarking different issues from labour to environment (Galbreath, 2006). Sector specific standards followed, successful examples including the Marine and the Forest Stewardship Council (Doh et al., 2010).

It has been doubted whether codes and standards are actually implemented by participating MNEs on a regular and worldwide basis (Voegtlin & Pless, 2014). Critics also refer to the lack of sanctions and a lack of financial commitments in many cases (van Tulder & Kolk, 2001). In addition standards may fail to address country-specific problems that are exacerbated by unsuitable CSR policies (Wiig & Kolstad, 2010). On the other hand, it has been argued international certifiable standards improve environmental MNE policies in emerging economies that lack the fundamental regulations necessary for environmental preservation (Christmann & Taylor, 2006). This notion has been supported by Christmann (2004) who observed a positive relationship between global CSR strategies and an improved environmental responsibility. Dögl and Holtbrügge (2014) similarly recommend that MNEs ought to standardise their environmental CSR by adopting a global approach. These arguments are supported by an ongoing debate on universal norms and global criteria for businesses (Windsor, 2013).

It seems environmental responsibility is particularly suitable for a global approach because it avoids cultural complexity. From a strategic perspective the global approach seems to appeal to many businesses because it is an efficient method. It provides them with a certificate issued by a credible institution, signalling serious commitment to consumers across borders. As more competitors adopt a given standard, legitimacy concerns pressure the remaining corporations to follow (Matten & Moon, 2008).

Waddock (2008), upon examining the "emerging institutional infrastructure around corporate responsibility" (p. 87), expects in line with Lo et al. (2008) that two trends will most likely shape the future of global CSR standards: A consolidation and further standardisation of the many initiatives and certified standards that exist today, and an increased influence of Asian perspectives into what is globally understood as CSR. CSR is a concept that originated from the United States (Matten & Moon, 2008). Asian nations, besides their growing importance in trade, can and almost certainly will have an impact on CSR as an evolving concept, offering constructive and enriching contributions drawing on Eastern holistic traditions (Waddock, 2008).

4.1.2 Global leadership

The implications of diverse cultures on CSR strategy are manifold (McWilliams et al., 2006). From a global CSR perspective, the probably most relevant findings can be derived from a study that has been conducted by Waldman et al. (2006) as part of the "Global Leadership and Organizational Behavior Effectiveness (GLOBE) research program" (p. 825). The scholars present significant evidence for diverging CSR values among cultures. Upon examining over 500 firms from five continents, the researchers identified differences regarding managers' concerns for shareholder, stakeholders and communities. These could be related to cultural dimensions such as *institutional collectivism* and *power distance*.

For example, the empirically supported concept of power distance reflects "the extent to which it is believed that power should be unequally distributed in a culture" (p. 826). According to the findings by Waldman et al. (2006), managers from high power distance cultures devalued concerns for shareholder, stakeholders and communities compared to their colleagues from low power distance cultures.

This has several implications for strategic CSR management. While Waldman et al. (2006) did not measure actual CSR performance, it can be reasoned that decentralised CSR yields significantly diverging outcomes across cultures. On one side because shareholders, stakeholders and communities are valued differently by managers from different cultural backgrounds. On the other side it is indicated that managers will differ in their overall commitment towards their CSR policy. Given the importance of stakeholder relations, the decentralised approach could directly influence the performance of concerned subsidiaries.

Not only does this support a more standardised and centralised, i.e. global approach to CSR within a MNE. In fact Waldman et al. (2006) emphasise the importance of CEO leadership as a driver of commitment to CSR, a related vision and values that influence the conduct of subordinate managers. This view is supported by Galbreath (2009) who emphasises the importance of assigning CSR strategy to corporate executives. Fisher and Bonn (2007) hold such a move indicates a sincere commitment to responsible conduct.

While cultures seem to share fundamental beliefs of what is right (Chapple & Moon, 2007; Donaldson & Dunfee, 1999; Williams & Zinkin, 2010), they seem to differ with respect to the importance they attach to CSR in general and different CSR dimensions in particular. Multinationals should prioritise them strategically. Leaving fundamental decisions on CSR to the discretion of country managers may lead to substantial divergences.

4.1.3 Global consistency

Consistency and efficiency are two sides of the same coin. Since strategic implications differ, they will be treated separately, however. Consistency is deeply intertwined with certified standards. The development of global CSR at the head quarter ensures that the highest standard required in one location will be implemented in all subsidiaries. Exploiting weaker regulations is bound to draw criticism of inconsistency and double standards (Polonsky & Jevons, 2009).

This was observed by Reimann et al. (2012) who noticed that firms often exploited variations among countries, especially weaker standards in developing countries. Muller (2006) therefore argues that global CSR carriers the potential to trigger a process of upward harmonisation. By introducing the highest standard proscribed in one country worldwide, the locations that allow for lower standards will benefit over proportionally. Such an approach will likely be perceived as being pro-active and consistently (Jamali, 2010). On the other hand competitors who do not adopt to the improved standard could come under pressure (Christmann, 2004). As a result MNEs usually tend to imitate the CSR policy of their major competitors (Laudal, 2011). Both the effect of upward harmonisation and the positive role of certified standards are supported by empirical studies by Fortanier, Kolk, and Pinkse (2011) and, for the food industry, by Aguilera, Rupp, Williams, and Ganapathi (2007).

Consistency contributes to the building of a strong brand in the global market place. This may lead to competitive advantages and substantially decreases the risk of adverse media campaigns stirred by inconsistencies too (Meyer, 2004; Polonsky & Jevons, 2009). As Popoli (2011) argued, the internet age does not allow for brands to have too distinct CSR strategies in different locations since judgements of stakeholders will be based on information from all locations.

Similarly worldwide consistency with regards to environmental CSR positively relates to employer branding (Dögl & Holtbrügge, 2014). The advantages associated with a consistent CSR strategy have been further explored by Oikonomou et al. (2014). The key finding indicates that MNEs with a consistent CSR strategy financially outperform firms that sporadically or inconsistently engage in CSR. An important source of inconsistency mentioned by the scholars concerns subsidiaries that did not participate in the policy. From the perspective of a subsidiary, centralised and global CSR increases the internal acceptance and legitimacy of its operations at the head quarter (Kostova & Roth, 2002).

4.1.4 Efficiency

A key reason why companies internationalise is efficiency. A global strategy is chosen especially by firms that compete on the basis of efficiency (Inkpen & Ramaswamy, 2006). Efficiency in a CSR context is associated with saving costs, easing implementation and ensuring goal achievement (Logsdon & Wood, 2005; Muller, 2006).

Jain and De Moya (2013) show that MNEs operating in India exhibit a clear preference towards a global CSR strategy. Most CSR programs were found to be concerned with support for education, healthcare and environmental issues. Issues that are specific to the Indian context such as micro finance, empowerment of women and slum improvement were rarely observed. Unfortunately the authors do not further investigate whether the issues associated with the global strategy were indeed applied to all host countries.

From a head quarter perspective Bondy and Starkey (2014) examined the CSR strategy of UK-based MNEs. In this case, a strong majority of 90 percent applied a global approach towards CSR during its decision making process. Here the senior management creates a draft, requests feedback from key stakeholders and sends the finalised version to the subsidiaries.

The global strategy would allow for no or only little changes in the host country. However, this time Bondy and Starkey (2014) observed only a minority of 20 percent of the MNEs to stick to the global approach. This is consistent with a study conducted by Jamali (2010) where the majority of MNE subsidiary managers implemented CSR within global guidelines.

Managers from the minority that followed the standardised program referred to the Global Compact and similar initiatives, indicating that the process of implementation resulted from a strategic choice for global CSR. In addition to environmental and corruption issues, elements that were deemed universal included "community development, education, welfare, health and safety" (Bondy & Starkey, 2014, p. 16). This is interesting because communities usually require different support across countries and therefore is considered to be a local CSR issue. The persisting lack of comprehensive definitions can not be overstated. Bondy and Starkey (2014) allow for local adaptation and, since communities can be addressed in every host country, categorise the issue accordingly.

On the other hand, Husted and Allen (2006) defined global CSR as being demanded by global stakeholders, for example, human rights and the environment. Empirical research revealed MNEs that adopt a global strategy for their products tend to apply the same strategy towards their CSR policy. Global issues seem to appeal to companies which also standardise other processes within the firm. This can be interpreted as another step towards efficiency, since the company invests less in additional processes and might therefore have a stronger impact on the issue.

In this regard Muller (2006) compared subsidiaries from European car manufacturers. The industry is characterised by high integration and comes under pressure for relocating produc- tion centres. Hence, the car manufacturer would develop a global CSR strategy. This strategy corresponds not only to his organisational strategy but allows for economies of scale.

Surprisingly, evidence suggested that CSR performance was positively related to a subsidi- ary's autonomy. In fact the more autonomous subsidiaries did not tailor their CSR policies to the host country, instead following the policy of the head quarter and its CSR policy voluntar- ily. Thereby Muller (2006) contributes to global CSR strategy by proposing that "firms may use a 'soft hand' approach that induces subsidiaries to adopt practices which they might resist under duress" (p. 196). According to these findings, successful CSR strategies involve the centralised process of designing the CSR policy, and the process of implementing it within autonomous subsidiaries.

Muller's (2006) finding is supported by Kostova and Roth (2002) who determined that subsidiaries exhibit an increased commitment towards policy implementation when trust and identification with the parent company grew. Tension seems to arise between *centralised control* and *trust*, which could explain the fact that both Jamali (2010), Bondy and Starkey (2014) found the process of CSR implementation to be less centralised.

Not only the organisational strategy influences the degree to which global CSR is adopted. Yang and Rivers (2009) argue that the dependency of a subsidiary increases conformity and therefore the adoption of global CSR programs. From an ownership perspective Salomon and Wu (2012) found that wholly-owned subsidiaries tend to conform with the parent company, while joined ventures tend to imitate practices of local firms. This indicates organisational configurations may favour global CSR practises as long as a subsidiary is tightly linked to the parent company, in consideration of the autonomy necessary in the field of CSR implementation.

4.1.5 Critical summary

Global CSR builds on self-regulation and emerging universal norms. These provide a MNE with consistency and efficiency, while upward harmonisation increases global standards which support developing countries. Empirical research indicates that global CSR is a widely shared approach. This is especially true with regard to environmental responsibility (Christmann, 2004; Dögl & Holtbrügge, 2014; Sharfman et al., 2004). Furthermore, education, safety, and human rights tend to be found among global CSR issues (Bondy & Starkey, 2014). The global organisational strategy in the product market seemingly favours global CSR (Husted & Allen, 2006). Similarly global CSR is popular among MNEs that build a strong and visible brand (Polonsky & Jevons, 2009).

On the other hand, a wide range of critics hold that the notion of CSR involves sensitivity towards societal differences arising from culture, institutions and the stage of development (Bondy & Starkey, 2014; Matten & Moon, 2008; Robertson, 2009). Therefore the standardised approach has been criticised for being not universal but ethically imperialistic and overweening (Logsdon & Wood, 2005). Robertson (2009) summarised this critique by referring to global CSR as an inappropriate and ill-fated attitude that disrespects relevant country characteristics ranging from culture to society and politics.

4.2 Local CSR

Over time societies develop as they differ among each other. It should be reiterated that CSR, according to Carroll (1979), encompasses the "discretionary expectations that society has of organizations at a given point in time" (p. 500). The diverging societal expectations can be linked to differences between cultures (Freeman & Hasnaoui, 2011; Waldman et al., 2006), the stage of economic development (Robertson, 2009; van Tulder & Kolk 2001; Waldman et al., 2006) and the institutional environment (Doh & Guay, 2006; Lo et al., 2008; Matten & Moon, 2008). Accordingly it is argued that the legitimacy of a CSR policy depends on the extent to which it adapts to country specific idiosyncrasies (Prieto-Carrón, Lund-Thomsen, Chan, Muro, & Bhushan, 2006). Longsdon and Wood (2005) thus describe the multi-domestic CSR strategy as being characterised by the "acceptance of and conformity to local laws and standards and a significant amount of autonomy for local management" (p. 57).

The local approach is founded in *institutional pressure* as well as *local stakeholder relations*. They are the main drivers that demand responsiveness of the subsidiary. The strategic advantages that come with a local approach are *legitimacy* and *efficacy*. Legitimacy is vital for successful operations and depends on the perception of the local stakeholders. Efficacy denotes the success of a tailored CSR policy in that it has a positive impact on the addressee. These aspects are interrelated and build on the assumption the MNE operates in multiple countries that differ among each other. The local or decentralised approach answers to high pressure for local responsiveness, yet it forgoes the benefits of global integration.

4.2.1 Institutional pressure

Institutional theory is widely considered to be a useful approach to international CSR (Doh & Guay, 2006; Husted & Allen, 2006; Matten & Moon, 2008; Tan & Wang, 2011; Salomon & Wu, 2012; Young & Makhija, 2014). By institutional theory CSR is framed as a legitimacy-seeking, and therefore strategic activity (Hamprecht & Schwarzkopf, 2014; Jamali, 2010). According to Kostova and Zaheer (1999), legitimacy denotes "the acceptance of the organiza-tion by its environment" which in turn is "vital for organizational survival and success" (p. 64).

Institutional theory builds on the assumption legitimacy is gained "across national borders through regulative, normative, and cognitive processes" (Jamali, 2010, p. 184). The cross-border perspective is ensured by the consideration of "national, cultural, and institutional contexts" (Matten & Moon, 2008, p. 406). Subsequently the perspective of a MNE subsidiary with the ability to develop a locally responsive CSR program is taken. In addition, it will be assumed that the subsidiary operates in a host country which carries characteristics that are distinct from the home country.

In principle this subsidiary needs to "conform to the parent firm's strategy, mission, policy, and procedures" (Yang & Rivers, 2009, p. 158). This *internal pressure* conflicts with *external pressure*. External pressure results from the institutional context of the host country, namely laws, rules, rights, norms, values and beliefs (Salomon & Wu, 2012; Young & Makhija, 2014). The inherent tension between the need for internal and external legitimacy faced by the subsidiary is denoted as *institutional duality* and is supported by empirical evidence (e.g., Hillman & Wan, 2005).

Yang and Rivers (2009) propose internal pressure decreases when the subsidiary is less dependent on the head quarter, and even more so in case the head quarter faces legitimacy issues in the host country. A subsidiary accordingly engages in local CSR initiatives as soon as external pressure outweighs the internal pressure. Large subsidiaries, for example, are less dependent and more visible and therefore more likely to face higher pressures for local responsiveness at the same time (Delmas & Toffel, 2004; Hillman & Wan, 2005). Jamali (2010) consistently notes that subsidiaries that hold decisive competencies such as manufacturing tend to pursue a local CSR strategy. Downstream activities such as marketing and services reversely coincide with less attention to local strategies.

A strong institutional framework in the host country has been found to be associated with an increase in CSR in general (Chapple & Moon, 2007; Zhao, Park, & Zhou, 2014) and local CSR in particular (Yang & Rivers, 2009). Consistently Young and Makhija (2014) present evidence for a positive relationship between local CSR and strong institutions, existing regulations and the rule of law. Luo (2006) distinguished between ethical codes released (arguably a global CSR strategy) and philanthropic contributions (a local CSR strategy) made by MNE subsidiaries in China. A clear relationship was established between an increase in perceived corruption and a decrease of the local CSR strategy.

Lo et al. (2008) compared the regulatory framework in the US and China in regards to consumer protection. MNEs responded to higher standards in the US by differentiating their consumer-related CSR initiatives between the two countries. Interestingly when it came to employee and environment oriented CSR, no differences were observed between the two countries. While institutional theory is a useful concept to determine diverging expectations across countries, not all of these have to remain static. Differences support the approach of a local CSR strategy. At the same time, Lo et al. (2008) note that these differences – at least some of them – may decrease in the long run. Companies that pursue a local approach have to be vigilant about a possible convergence between Western and Chinese CSR.

This perception is supported by Zhao et al. (2014). As the Chinese environment changes dramatically, MNEs increasingly encounter public crises. The authors attribute this to underdeveloped local stakeholder relations and increasing local competition between MNEs, "a typical phenomenon in transition economies" where "new regulations emerge and enforcing them becomes more effective, and civil society actions increase" (p. 856). The risk for encountering a legitimacy crises is high when fierce competition forces the subsidiary to exploit institutional voids while stakeholders yield more power and increase their expectations. Zhao et al. (2014) conclude that a local strategy requires not a mere adjustment of CSR policies but a conscious stakeholder-orientation and continuing stakeholder dialogue to understand concerns and changing expectations.

4.2.2 Stakeholder relations

External pressures in the host country are deeply intertwined with local stakeholders (Park, Chidlow, & Choi, 2014). The dependency of the MNE subsidiary on its local stakeholders, particularly in an emerging market context, has been widely accepted (e.g., Park et al., 2014; Yang & Rivers, 2009; Young & Makhija, 2014). As it is argued by Frooman (1999), stakeholders use influencing strategies with a view of changing a behaviour of the firm, according to their interests. Especially customers and employees control relevant resources that allow them to influence the company. Hence not all stakeholders hold the same strategic importance (Jamali, 2008; Park & Ghauri, 2015).

Strategic stakeholder management involves identifying the salient stakeholder groups, understanding their demands and designing CSR strategies that satisfy them while considering the limited financial resources of the subsidiary. Out of a variety of stakeholders, consumers are the most salient stakeholders and a main driver of CSR (Park et al., 2014; Park & Ghauri, 2015). Accordingly, customer satisfaction has been described as the foundation of competitive advantages in host countries. Other stakeholders that were found to be of particular relevance include employees and local managers as well as NGOs (Park et al., 2014). Park and Ghauri (2015) additionally identified competitors to be a driving force behind increased local CSR in South Korea. While upward harmonisation has been considered to be a global phenomena, this finding indicates that a similar process exists on a country level in case subsidiaries manage their CSR policies on a local basis.

Once the relevant stakeholders have been identified, the subsidiary needs to identify and satisfy their demands. According to Bhattacharya, Korschun, and Sen (2009), a strategy for successful stakeholder relationships will be grounded in CSR initiatives that yield three distinct categories of benefits for a stakeholder group: Functional, psychosocial and value benefits. A functional benefit relates to tangible features of a product or an initiative, while psychosocial well-being refers to the intangible results of the former. Ideally, values foster trust as stakeholders identify with the initiative and the company that is associated with it.

These benefits which have been borrowed from marketing literature clearly depend on the perceptions of stakeholders. In turn perceptions may vary significantly among different cultures and the socio-economic development stages of host countries. In this regard, Lindgreen et al. (2009) emphasise that CSR strategies require a deep understanding of the addressee and local values. A lack of sensitivity and dialogue with stakeholders negatively impacts both the subsidiaries operations and local stakeholders.

4.2.3 Local suitability

While global CSR aims at gaining legitimacy by exhibiting consistency, local CSR is about adequate adaptation to country specific issues. A range of research emphasises the importance of the latter from a strategic perspective. Barin Cruz and Boehe (2010), for example, suggest that competitive advantages may be hardly derived from CSR unless the policy reflects local conditions. Young and Makhija (2014) expect that MNEs gain legitimacy depending on the degree of their responsiveness to the local requirements.

Benefits derived from legitimacy in the host country include a reduction of uncertainty (Park et al., 2014; Young & Makhija, 2014), mitigation of the liability of foreignness (Campbell et al., 2012; Yang & Rivers, 2009) and improved relationships with local stakeholders (Jamali,

2010; Reimann et al., 2012). Legitimacy is rooted in a perception of the specific CSR as being suitable. Suitability of CSR can be determined by the degree it considers idiosyncrasies of the host country, which are mainly socio-economic and cultural in nature.

Socio-economic problems in an emerging market vary as they can be related to "transition problems (Eastern Europe), extreme growth rates (China), or high inequality (Brazil and India)" (Barin Cruz & Boehe, 2010, p. 243). More specifically prevalent issues in the Brazilian context are the Amazon river, high inequality and street children (Barin Cruz & Boehe, 2010). In a Lebanese context Jamali (2010) refers to an ambitious governmental action plan aimed at reducing the profound regional disparity in poverty distribution. She argued that MNE subsidiaries operating in this country ought to address precisely this problem with their local CSR strategy. Any well-conceived contribution in this context would support governmental efforts, improve the macroeconomic situation and display concern for the host country. In an Indian context local CSR would be concerned with issues such as micro finance, women's empowerment and slum improvement (Jain & De Moya, 2013).

Cultural differences are not less important. Without going into detail, one example given by Donaldson and Dunfee (1999) on the Indian context attempts to illustrate what responsiveness implies. In India it is not unusual to reward employees by promising employment opportunities for one of their children. The company expresses its appreciation of the long-term employee, while the loyalty of the latter contributes to the career prospects of his child. This clearly conflicts with Western values such as individualism and egalitarianism. However, from the view of Indian society this implies respect for traditional values, long-term relationships and the concept of the extended family. Responsiveness in its cultural sense therefore implies an understanding of and respect for local culture and values.

4.2.4 Efficacy

Results from a cross-country field research by Robertson (2009) supports the notion CSR-related expectations and understandings vary significantly among different countries. Based on the conclusion of Bhattacharya et al. (2009) "that stakeholders assess the efficacy of CSR initiatives" (p. 268), evidence suggests that strategic CSR needs to be tailored to specific host country issues. In oil-rich Angola, for example, MNE subsidiaries from the energy sector strategically focus on environmental issues and hiring of local employees as a way to ensure contracts (Wiig & Kolstad, 2010). Evidence from an emerging market context by Park et al.

(2014) points to the importance of building long-term relationships with both governmental bodies and local communities.

Reimann et al. (2012) conducted one of the most comprehensive studies available on the question of responsiveness and efficacy. The large-scale, cross-industry study involved more than 200 MNEs from Eastern Europe, Asia and Latin America, thus providing highly valuable insights into the relationship between local CSR and local stakeholders in emerging economies.

First of all the authors determined a positive relationship between working performance of employees and the two local CSR initiatives observed – increased working conditions and increased community development efforts. The link between employee performance and community development is interesting for it is not directly related. Employees might be proud of their companies' efforts or identify with the values that are associated with community support (Reimann et al., 2012). From a cultural perspective it could be argued that Asian societies tend to be less individualistic than industrialised nations.

Secondly relationships with local authorities improved only in case the subsidiary supported community development projects. This indicates the observation supported by Bhattacharya et al. (2009) that an individual stakeholder group has to be addressed with a specific CSR issue. Local CSR does not necessarily enhance local legitimacy towards every stakeholder group, even though specific initiatives can yield significant benefits for the company (e.g., increased employee performance). Another important finding of Reimann et al. (2012) regards the fact that from an organisational perspective the middle management of the subsidiary constitutes a key driver behind CSR policies, at least in the emerging market context examined.

The observation of the importance of community development as a CSR issue is interesting. At first it is an issue that necessitates local approach. Furthermore, contributions are likely to make a huge difference since the majority of MNE subsidiaries today can be found in developing and emerging markets. Actually community development seems to be a CSR issue that increasingly gains positive attention (e.g., Lai Cheng & Ahmad, 2010; Porter & Kramer, 2011). Porter and Kramer (2006) refer to highly successful partnerships between MNEs and local communities where "the success of the company and the success of the community become mutually reinforcing" (p. 89). Yang and Rivers (2009) support this idea noting that a successful subsidiary should move from initial impact mitigation towards a social partnership that is grounded in the potential of businesses to become a driver of social advancement.

Equally interesting in this regard is the observation by Waldman et al. (2006). Managers from wealthier countries were less inclined to emphasise the community dimension of CSR which probably relates to the existence of welfare states in industrialised countries. Reversely it has been reported in an Asian context that the local community is among the most prominent CSR issues (Chapple & Moon, 2005). From another perspective, Waldman et al. (2006) indicated that local managers should not be assigned with the CSR management process whereas Reimann et al. (2012) note the positive influence of the local management. Whether this contradiction might be explained by methodology – Waldman et al. (2006) examined attitudes, not actual performance, while Reimann et al. (2012) considered performance, not attitudes – or whether this indicates a recent change could be subject to further investigation.

4.2.5 Critical summary

Altogether the main driver for local CSR is institutional and stakeholder pressure arising from the host country (Tan & Wang, 2011). The responsive CSR strategy positively influences stakeholder-relations on which the company relies (Yang and Rivers, 2009; Young & Makhija, 2014). In order to manage these relations strategically, the subsidiary will identify salient stakeholders initially (Park et al., 2014) and consider their perceptions of specific CSR issues (Bhattacharya et al., 2009). Responsiveness takes into account significant cross-country differences and tailors initiatives accordingly. The suitability and efficacy of its initiatives tends to result in increased legitimacy, reduced uncertainty and liability of foreignness.

Reimann et al. (2012) contributed in several ways to the understanding of local CSR. First, not every CSR issue influences relevant stakeholders. Second, not all CSR issues that influence a stakeholder group are directly related to this group. In particular, community development efforts seem to be of significant importance in an emerging market context. Third, the local management was found to be a key driver behind CSR efforts.

On the other hand, critics hold that local CSR will be fragmented, reactive, and exploit lower standards in developing countries (Jamali, 2010; Muller, 2006). As initiatives remain within the realm of the subsidiary, no process of organisational learning can be expected to leverage experiences globally (Barin Cruz & Boehe, 2010). If responsiveness to local culture is taken to an extreme, managers may subscribe to ethical relativism to an extent where no universal values will be left to judge an action (Longsdon & Wood, 2005).

4.3 Transnational CSR

The transnational model has been proposed by Bartlett and Ghoshal (1998) as an answer to "the need for simultaneously achieving global efficiency, national responsiveness, and the ability to develop and exploit knowledge on a worldwide basis" (p. 65). On the organisational level this implies a structure with interdependencies among different subsidiaries as well as individual subsidiaries and the head quarter (Harzing, 2000).

Obviously, this ambitious structure requires substantial resources and time to develop because of its complexity (Morschett et al., 2009). However, given the persisting limitations of both global and local CSR, several attempts have been made to develop a "hybrid strategy" along the transnational model. These attempts are grounded in evidence suggesting that neither exclusively global nor local CSR strategies provide a lasting solution to MNEs (Stahl & Sully de Luque, 2014). Transnational CSR accordingly "balances standardization with customization to reap the advantages of adapting to local contexts, while maintaining consistency with the overall business strategy" (Jain & De Moya, 2013, p. 208).

Husted and Allen (2006) were among the first who suggested that strategic CSR would have to respond to both, pressures for integration and responsiveness. The scholars developed a global versus local model, missing the opportunity to include a transnational strategy. This was criticised by Bondy and Starkey (2014) who complained transnational strategies are passed over in most of the existing literature. While this is true, it can be assumed that this research gap at least partially stems from the lack of definitions and accepted frameworks.

Concepts identical or very similar to transnational CSR have been termed "hybrid" (Logsdon & Wood, 2002), "integrated" (Bondy & Starkey, 2014), "glocal" (Jain & De Moya, 2013), and "diluted" (Jamali, 2010). This might be explained by the fact that not all research draws on the typology of Bartlett and Ghoshal (1998), although such an approach had been proposed by scholars (Arthaud-Day, 2005; Logsdon & Wood, 2002, 2005) and formed the "dominant theoretical approach" to international CSR since (Chapple & Moon, 2007, p. 184).

The literature concerned with the transnational CSR strategy may be categorised into three approaches: *Global business citizenship* is a theory that draws on the concepts of *organisational learning* and *integrative social contracts theory*. The former is an advantage forgone by global and local strategies. The latter fits into the transnational approach for it considers local values without dismissing the notion of universal values. From another perspective, the *conceptual framework* as well as the findings on *balanced stakeholder demands* indicate that many subsidiares exhibit *tendencies* towards a more integrated or responsive CSR strategy. Finally, *transverse CSR management* integrates the aforementioned strategies in a complex, yet well conceived manner by creating strong linkages between the headquarter, business units and stakeholders in different host countries.

4.3.1 Global business citizenship

The probably closest application of the transnational model to CSR strategy can be found in Logsdon and Wood (2005). Their *global business citizenship* model describes a CSR strategy that distinguishes between cases that require a uniform approach and other situations where adaptation and sensitivity becomes necessary. Noting that the model was referred to as "hybrid strategy" by the scholars earlier (Logsdon and Wood, 2002), clarity may justify the henceforth designation as transnational CSR.

The adoption of the transnational CSR strategy passes through four stages. In the beginning the global MNE adopts a code of conduct. The subsidiaries implement the code locally. The third step involves analysis and experimentation. Pressure for responsiveness increases as ethical certainty decreases. Indeed conflict may arise between the global code and its local application. At this stage the fourth step requires organisational learning, involving the head quarter as well as its subsidiaries. Subsequently the MNE adjusts its CSR policy as "the global and local perspectives correct and inform one another" (Arthaud-Day, 2005, p. 11).

The development of a global code may involve global certified standards and international CSR initiatives. In addition Logsdon and Wood (2005) refer to the concept of *hypernorms,* which was developed to avoid the two accusations which are cultural imperialism and ethical relativism that have been levelled at the global and local approach to ethics (Arthaud-Day, 2005; Logsdon & Wood, 2005; Stahl & Sully de Luque, 2014).

4.3.2 Integrative social contracts theory

The idea of hypernorms is based on integrative social contracts theory. This theory attempts to overcome ethical relativism in international business. Donaldson and Dunfee (1999) proposed the idea of hypernorms which are universal, authentic beliefs and values accepted and shared across cultures. Examples of hypernorms include "fundamental human rights or basic prescriptions common to most major religions" (p. 52). The second key concept is termed *moral free space*. It respects "unique, but strongly held, cultural beliefs" (p. 53) that do not conflict with hypernorms, at least not contradict them.

The concept builds on the observation that, for example, bribery is condemned in all religious texts and by philosophers from very different schools of thought. Additionally Donaldson and Dunfee (1999) found managers in highly corrupt countries to justify their actions in ways that indicated bribery was not their authentic belief. In fact, the act of bribery violated a hyper-norm. On the other hand, respecting cultural differences across countries is vital for business as well as ethics. By applying this framework Donaldson and Dunfee (1999) argue the company will be "acknowledging both universal moral limits and the ability of communities to set moral standards of their own" (p. 50). This "major contribution" to international CSR (Carroll, 2004, p. 115) has been supported by Doh et al. (2010) who refer to the concept of hypernorms as "the most creative response" (p. 491) to tensions that arise when navigating across different cultures. The model allows for responsiveness without dismissing the notion of universal foundations of ethics.

4.3.3 A conceptual CSR framework

The global business citizenship and the concept of hypernorms may serve as a guideline. However, they neglect the fact not all subsidiaries will be equal in terms of size, competencies and stakeholder demands. This aspect was rather irrelevant in the global and local strategy. On the other hand, the transnational approach relies on relationships between subsidiaries, taking into account their differences. As noted by Egri and Ralston (2008), the large majority – three out of four papers on international CSR – take an empirical approach. Hence the following theoretical framework represents a highly valuable contribution towards an under-standing of the strategic decision-making on a subsidiary level.

The arguably most comprehensive attempt to unify existing theories into a conceptual CSR framework has been undertaken by Hah and Freeman (2014). It builds on three assumptions, namely: Global and local CSR respectively carry strengths and weaknesses; the approaches are not mutually exclusive, allowing for a subsidiary to find the ideal balance between global and local CSR; the strategically required balance is a result of internal and external determi-nants. At the same time this kind of approach supports the notion of Bondy and Starkey (2014) who argue a purely transnational strategy might not be possible.

From the subsidiary perspective in a host country internal and external determinants are mainly constituted by *isomorphic pressure*. This concept is borrowed from institutional theory. It describes the legitimacy seeking efforts of the subsidiary that involve the imitation of policies and practices that are expected by internal or external actors (Kostova & Zaheer, 1999, p. 71). Isomorphic pressure to build *internal legitimacy* results in a global CSR strategy, while pressure for *external legitimacy* fosters a local CSR strategy. Internal legitimacy has been defined as "the acceptance and approval of an organizational unit by the other units within the firm and, primarily, by the parent company" (Kostova & Zaheer, 1999, p. 72). Capital, knowledge and other resources are distributed mainly by the parent company. Therefore high dependency of a subsidiary increases internal pressure. The countervailing force of external pressure is related to increased size, visibility and dependency on local stakeholders.

Institutional duality, the simultaneous pressure for internal and external legitimacy, is a common conflict faced by an oversea subsidiary (Kostova & Zaheer, 1999). Jamali (2010) summarised these observations into four major impacting variables regarding the CSR strategy of the subsidiary: The resource dependency on the parent company, its strategic role in the MNE network, its relevance for the host country and specific competencies. These variables influence the two pressures that, in turn, influence the *degree* to which a rather global or local CSR approach is being taken.

From a similar perspective Tan and Wang (2011) observed that subsidiaries under pressure from internal and external forces will have to decide for an ethical strategy. In addition to institutional duality, the subsidiary encounters a *logic dilemma*. This dilemma "emerges when activities which aim to satisfy logic expectations and requirements in the home country contradict the logic counterparts in the host country" (p. 377). The contradicting expectations can be met in four distinct ways, or ethical strategies, which are determined by *CSR ingrainedness* and the level of *ethical pressure* in the host country. CSR ingrainedness refers to the "degree to which a corporation prioritizes CSR in its strategy and systematically and routinely incorporates CSR into its daily practices" (p. 378). Ethical pressure refers to the degree to which local norms and the logic expectations of the host country are demanded by local stakeholders. These four possible strategies are denoted as *defiance, compliance, camouflage,* and *negotiation*.

Defiance is a strategy which emerges when CSR ingrainedness is high and ethical pressure weak. The subsidiary has a developed CSR strategy building on values that are embraced by the host country. Reversely, compliance describes a strategy where CSR ingrainedness is low, but ethical pressure in the host country tends to demand certain values that the subsidiary is willing to subscribe to. Both situations imply a solution which is beneficial for both sides. Defiance is a strategy often adopted by a MNE originating in a developed country where higher regulations and stakeholder demands resulted in high CSR ingrainedness. Alternatively, compliance can be observed in cases of emerging-market based MNEs that increasingly enter European and American markets. In order to respond to regulations and gain legitimacy it is imperative for them to subscribe to higher regulations and stakeholder expectations.

Camouflage and negotiation can be difficult in ethical and economic terms. Camouflage strategy is an attempt of the subsidiary to respond to high CSR ingrainedness and strong ethical pressure. It describes an attempt to retain yet hide the domestic core values in order to maintain legitimacy internally without loosing it externally. Tan and Wang (2011) exemplify this strategy through the failed attempt of Google to enter the Chinese market. The company had to accept internet filters and censor search results, while advancing the idea of an uncensored net at home. As pressure grew in the United States, it finally had to pull out of the China.

Negotiation is a strategy where both CSR ingrainedness and ethical pressure is weak. The absence of any type of stronger pressure implies that the subsidiary may tend to exploit weak regulations. A typical case is a developed-country based MNE that enters a developing country with few regulations and low institutional pressure. Because this MNE did not develop a CSR program in the home market, it is even more unlikely to do so abroad; its core values are subject to changes and will be renounced easily.

Hah and Freeman (2014) hold that their model is designed especially for an emerging market. However, it is not clear why this limitation should apply. Rather it can be argued this framework combines two highly valuable approaches which will facilitate future research towards an evolving international CSR model. Similarly the authors emphasise the framework may be useful in smaller emerging economies like South East Asia. While this certainly holds true, none of the scholars who contributed to the framework emphasised such a context. Kostova and Zaheer (1999), Jamali (2010), as well as Tan and Wang (2011) examined MNEs from an IB perspective in general and from an institutional perspectives in particular. The probably greatest weakness of the framework lies in the underdeveloped link between institutional duality and the logic dilemma: Do they differ? And if they do so, to what extent? This requires an explanation. If they do not, a single term should be provided in order to really merge the concepts summarised in the framework.

4.3.4 Balancing stakeholder demands

Scholars who examine attempts of transnational CSR strategies have been largely critical because the trade-offs between global and local stakeholders become very clear in the process. Their observations support the notion that this approach constitutes rather a balancing act than a fully-fledged stand-alone strategy. Husted and Allen (2006) for example determined the organisational strategy (global, local, transnational) of MNEs operating in Mexico. They expected organisational strategy to be independent from CSR strategy, for the latter evolves along global and local pressures that are distinct from the product-market.

The transnational CSR proposed by Husted and Allen (2006) emerges as a result of "a case-by-case analysis" of prevalent stakeholders (p. 848). That is, some CSR issues will be managed globally, while others arise locally. As this is an arguably simplistic assumption that neglects the hybrid idea, their study provided one of the very first empirical insights into strategic CSR management. According to the findings, Global MNEs did not engage in local CSR activities. Both, multidomestic and transnational MNEs, i.e. the two types that are locally responsive, engaged in global and local CSR initiatives – a transnational CSR approach, according to the definition of the authors. Husted and Allen (2006) criticised the global approach in particular for failing to consider local stakeholders. The authors offer no further differentiation between the local and transnational approach, and their descriptive paper does not explain how decisions regarding CSR strategy were taken by the management.

This challenge was addressed by Jamali (2010) who studied the CSR strategy of MNE subsidiaries in Lebanon. The majority of subsidiary managers reported CSR themes to be developed at the regional office before being adapted to and implemented in the Lebanese context. While this indicates a transnational approach, Jamali (2010) doubts the usefulness of mere adaptation because it ignores priorities of the addressees. The policy neither involved local stakeholders in the development of the CSR program nor did it pay attention to country-specific problems.

Jamali (2010) refers to standardised CSR that is subsequently transferred to subsidiaries as being "diluted" and "detached from local needs/demands in host countries, anchored in a predominant preoccupation with garnering symbolic-type legitimacy" (p. 196). The MNE is aware of the need to gain local legitimacy, yet it does not embrace the full potential of CSR by involving salient local stakeholders. In addition only three out of ten subsidiaries reported on CSR policies that were connected to their core competencies. This approach has been suggested, for example, by Porter and Kramer (2002, 2006, 2011). Connecting CSR to core competencies of a firm convincingly indicates that a company adopts CSR as a strategy – an opportunity missed by the majority of the subsidiaries in Lebanon. Jamali (2010) further points out no measuring mechanisms have been established to understand the actual impact of a CSR program.

Although it can be concluded that these observations have been influenced by the fact the Lebanese market is rather small and does not carry the importance of other markets in the region such as Turkey, similar observations by Bondy and Starkey (2014), as well as Jain and De Moya (2013) indicate that in fact many MNEs follow similar approaches. In the case of Jain and De Moya (2013), websites of subsidiaries operating in India were examined on the basis of global and local CSR themes addressing global concerns and country-specific issues respectively. Similarly to Jamali (2010), the scholars highlight the importance of considering the Indian context for strategically developing CSR policies. Jain and De Moya (2013) investigated the extent to which subsidiaries of MNEs renowned for their social responsibility reaped the benefits that come with the transnational strategy. The authors emphasise that they expected subsidiaries to adopt their companies overall CSR strategy to the Indian context.

Out of 38 MNEs operating in India, only seven subsidiaries engaged in this type of transnational CSR, with a majority of 18 subsidiaries exhibiting a purely global CSR approach. Most Indian subsidiaries displayed the same CSR content that was part of the MNEs main website, with no case of Hindi language content. Hence Jain and De Moya (2013) arrive at a conclusion that resembles Jamali's (2010) remarks: MNE subsidiaries "are losing the opportunity to engage local stakeholders by failing to localize … their CSR efforts" (Jain & De Moya, 2013, p. 222).

The authors assume the prevalence of global CSR to be connected to the weak institutional framework. In fact, no official guidelines or reporting standards on CSR can be found in this important Asian country. The scholars apparently provide evidence for the widely held assumption of a positive relationship between CSR and institutional regulations (e.g., Lo et al., 2008; Yang & Rivers, 2009; Young & Makhija, 2014). It can be reasoned that both the importance of a market and its institutional regulation strongly influence the extent to which local stakeholders are included in CSR policies.

This assumption is supported by the findings of Bondy and Starkey (2014). The authors conducted interviews with managers from UK-based MNEs that develop transnational CSR policies. Although during the implementation process a majority of companies encouraged adaptation to local requirements, the outcomes mostly resembled global CSR approaches. As a result, Bondy and Starkey (2014) "question whether integrated strategies are possible even conceptually" (p. 19). From a cultural perspective it is argued that in many cases Western ideas were deemed universal. From an organisational perspective the scholars blame a lack of consultation between the senior management and seemingly non-influential stakeholders for a rather centralised result. However, the paper carries the important limitation that these stakeholders, as well as subsidiary managers, were not interviewed to further advance this argument. It is important to reiterate the repeatedly provided evidence for stakeholder influence especially on subsidiaries (e.g., Park et al., 2014; Park & Ghauri, 2015; Reimann et al., 2012; Yang & Rivers, 2009). In line with the model proposed by Hah and Freeman (2014) it can be assumed that a variety of impacting variables lead to *tendencies* towards global or local strategies. While many of the observations seem to indicate that MNEs forgo advantages of responsive CSR, it should be noted there is a realistic possibility that the mentioned complexity at least partially favours such an outcome.

4.3.5 Transverse CSR management

While Jamali (2010) conducted interviews with subsidiary managers, Bondy and Starkey (2014) were interested in a head quarter perspective. The advantage of these approaches mainly lies in the rather large set of MNEs involved. At the same time the main limitation of these studies is the lack of understanding the whole organisation and multiple perspectives. Accepting the limitation of examining only two MNEs, Barin Cruz and Pedrozo (2009) as well as Barin Cruz and Boehe (2010) tried to capture both the head quarter and subsidiary perspective with regards to CSR strategies.

The authors chose two retail MNEs from France and their Brazilian subsidiary for their case study. This setting captures a common situation where the head quarter is located in a developed country and the subsidiary faces the challenges and opportunities that characterise emerging markets. Even more interestingly, the retail and food industry is characterised by a higher CSR performance than other industries (Strike, Gao, & Bansal, 2006). Thus a limited but highly relevant field of study was chosen to derive a transnational framework.

Barin Cruz and Pedrozo (2009) derive two major recommendations from their observations. First, large MNEs are well advised to establish a CSR department. The main task of the department is to develop, control and to coordinate the CSR policy. This might require more resources and take more time to develop, yet unlike rather uncoordinated efforts a tangible outcome and continuous improvements can be expected. Second, the different departments within the MNE engage in CSR activities that will be linked to each other by a transverse structure. CSR projects inform each other and with regards to challenges, opportunities and changes, involving the different subsidiaries and head quarter simultaneously. Such an approach is supported by the idea of gaining competitive advantages by integrating CSR into the core business as suggested by Porter and Kramer (2002, 2006, 2011).

Moving beyond the case study, Barin Cruz and Boehe (2010) conceptualise an approach that describes the transverse CSR management: An entity involving "(1) top managers, (2) representatives of functional areas, (3) representatives of subsidiary units, and (4) representatives of external stakeholders" (p. 251). Obviously, the top management ensures the global coordination, while the subsidiaries tailor the CSR policy to their host country needs. The involvement of functional areas such as the human resource, production and logistics department ensures the linkage to the core business. Finally, by proposing the involvement of external stakeholders, the authors include a group whose marginalisation has been criticised in the studies of Jamali (2010), Jain and De Moya (2013), and Bondy and Starkey (2014).

By means of *hierarchical*, *relational*, *cultural*, and *collaborative* mechanisms, four challenges can be addressed: The challenge for global integration, local responsiveness, worldwide learning from local CSR and, eventually, competitive advantages based on CSR. The hierarchical mechanism resembles global, centralised processes. The relational mechanism refers to the internal inclusion of departments and employees. The cultural mechanism denotes attempts to create an organisational culture, awareness for and identification with socially responsible goals that create value for both business and society. After all, the collaborative mechanism involves external stakeholders, especially local community programs and partnerships with NGOs, providing legitimacy and competitive advantages to the firm.

Hamprecht and Schwarzkopf (2014) report a case where a small subsidiary that has been exposed to a large number of external stakeholders started developing a CSR initiative. The head quarter, though sceptical in the beginning, soon leveraged the local experience globally. This illustrates the importance of bottom-up linkages in a MNE which do not exist under the global or local strategy. The transverse CSR strategy combines many valuable recommendations, although no additional studies indicate that MNEs embrace this concept. This concept is closest to the transnational ideal, yet it is probably the most challenging proposal in terms of realisation.

4.3.6 Critical summary

Transnational CSR attempts to earn the benefits related to global and local CSR simultaneously. A range of studies remains critical towards its feasibility, citing evidence that transnational CSR tends to remain a diluted version of the global approach (Bondy & Starkey, 2014; Jain & De Moya, 2013; Jamali, 2010). On the other hand, several drivers towards both increased global and local CSR require creative answers. The global business citizenship model by Logsdon and Wood (2002, 2005) as well as transverse CSR management by Barin Cruz and Pedrozo (2009) and Barin Cruz and Boehe (2010) provide a promising foundation for a start. Allowing for varying degrees of global and local CSR in different subsidiaries, the Hah and Freeman (2014) combine important frameworks by Kostova and Zaheer (1999), Jamali (2010) as well as Tan and Wang (2011).

Clearly, this approach has the potential to overcome limitations of global and local CSR strategies. However, it remains an evolving concept that needs both theoretical and empirical development. From a managerial perspective, the transnational approach is more complex while promising greater advantages at the same time.

4.4 Influencing variables

It is tempting at this stage to recommend a transnational CSR strategy that overcomes the limitations of both global and local solutions. This could be justified by intensified pressure for global standardisation – e.g., the growing popularity of certified standards – and growing pressure for responsiveness – e.g., legitimacy crises in emerging markets. However, it has become equally clear that many MNEs fail to achieve this balance, according to the initial studies available. It could be argued not every MNE requires the same strategic configuration.

Hence, an increasing stream of IB literature does no longer solely examine the organisational CSR strategy. While Husted and Allen (2006) found no relationship between local CSR and "firm size, industry sector, or country of origin" (p. 846), others did (Lu et al., 2014; Strike et al., 2006). CSR policies are studied in relation to defined parameters with a view to understanding possible underlying patterns and their implications for strategy. So CSR with respect to distance, industry, and visibility will be discussed. This perspective contributes to strategic CSR by identifying impacting variables.

4.4.1 Distance

Distance has first been linked explicitly to international CSR strategies by Campbell et al. (2012). The concept refers to the degree of differences between the home and the host country. This has long been found helpful in predicting internationalisation processes of firms. Johanson and Vahlne (1977) described their concept of distance as being composed of "differences in language, education, business practices, culture, and industrial development" (p. 24). According to their observation in a Swedish context, companies would gradually increase their investments and their commitment to a new market. The more distant a market is, the more experience would be necessary for operations. CSR will be practised in the domestic market and gradually become part of subsidiaries abroad, according to this logic. Furthermore, experience allows for a suitable adaptation to host country needs (Campbell et al., 2012). This implies that, over time, subsidiaries could move from a global to a transnational CSR policy.

However, this is only one of several possibilities. Building on the framework of Kostova and Zaheer (1999), it has been assumed by Yang and Rivers (2009) that increased *institutional distance* fosters local CSR. That is, the greater the difference between the institutions of the home country and the host country, the less does a global CSR approach hold.

Institutional distance refers to the degree of differences between the regulatory and institutional environment of the domestic and the host country of a MNE (Kostova & Zaheer, 1999). As explained earlier, external pressure leads to an increase of local CSR. In this vein, CSR could help to lower distance. However, it might be noted that this relationship is difficult to observe: A set of developed-country MNEs could change CSR policies abroad because of lower regulations and low stakeholder pressure, as opposed to increased local responsiveness (Tan & Wang, 2011).

Another concept of distance, *cultural distance*, refers to "the assumptions, values, norms and beliefs shared by individuals in a society" (Campbell et al., 2012). According to findings by Luo (2006), higher cultural distance in China positively relates to ethical codes and negatively to philanthropic contributions. If this was to be generalisable, institutional and cultural distance would influence CSR responsiveness in contrary ways. Institutional distance would increase local, cultural distance decrease local CSR.

Using the CAGE model, Campbell et al. (2012) provide interesting insights in this regard. The CAGE model is applied to measure distances, including cultural, administrative (that is, institutional), geographic and economic distance. Examining the CSR policies of US-based bank subsidiaries, the scholars found significant evidence for a negative relation between local CSR and increased distance in all four dimensions of the model.

These findings carry several theoretical and practical implications. From a theoretical point of view, Campbell et al. (2012) used the concept of liability of foreignness (LOF) to predict an increase of local CSR in distant markets. This is in line with the reasoning of Yang and Rivers (2009). LOF refers to the "greater challenge to establish and maintain legitimacy in their host environments, compared to domestic firms, because of the stereotyping and different stand-ards applied to foreign firms by the host environment" (Kostova & Zaheer, 1999, p. 74). Obviously, an increase in CSR could increase legitimacy and provide the foreign firm with a valuable reputation.

On the other hand, Campbell et al. (2012) maintain that the willingness and ability of manag-ers to develop CSR strategies may decrease significantly in an unfamiliar environment. Willingness is negatively affected by a decreased identification with the host country, ability relates to experience similar to the concept of Johanson and Vahlne (1977). A lack of experi-ence in the host country may hamper efforts to successfully develop CSR policies. What is more, missing identification and experience abroad is contrasted with a good understanding of the home market. CSR is implemented at home more easily, more efficient and effective.

It could be argued the US-based banks faced lower regulations abroad which loosed pressures for CSR investments. This assumption is supported by the moderating variable – the high CSR reputation of a firm. Subsidiaries face higher expectations in case they already have a responsible reputation. Instead of relying on this reputation, consistency has to be exhibited in order to remain legitimate. The findings indicate that commitment to CSR policies varies between countries – a fact often overlooked by studies that choose a set of subsidiaries within one host country but different countries of origin.

The practical implication of this is that "the affiliate's reputation also significantly alters (weakens) the impact of CAGE distance on the likelihood of engaging in CSR" (Campbell et al., 2012, p. 100). Besides the US-context, the major limitation is the focus on the financial industry and bank subsidiaries. Banks may not cater to a wide range of private customers in highly distant developing countries. Stakeholder pressure could therefore decrease, while other industries experience a reverse pattern abroad.

4.4.2 Industry

It has been noted earlier some certified standards are industry-specific. Similarly, upward harmonisation is a process that mainly occurs within a given industry. According to Aguilera et al. (2007), an industry can often be described by specific regulations, norms and values. Competitors monitor the prevalent CSR practices of their industry as they understand the need to be perceived as legitimate. This legitimacy is largely derived from compliance with industry norms. Falling below these established standards is often associated with serious consequences such as bad publicity and a serious damage of reputation.

The assumption of diverging CSR strategies among different industries is supported by findings of Sweeney and Coughlan (2008). For example, car manufacturers as well as oil and gas companies emphasised environmental policies as their major CSR theme. On the other hand, retailers and the financial service sector emphasised customers and employees in their CSR policy. Within a given industry, Delmas and Toffel (2004) expect increased consolidation and high market concentration to accelerate the acceptance of CSR standards. High competition and few participants will lead to a standard that would not become accepted easily in a more fragmented industry. However, his study does not take into account the dynamics of international business and global competition.

Building on the above, several studies examined industry-specific CSR. Wiig and Kolstad (2010) selected the oil industry for their research in Angola. In the energy sector, and in particular in the context of developing countries, the authors warn that local CSR in Africa may exacerbate existing problems arising from illegitimate institutions. The CSR initiative that addresses local authorities is hardly socially responsible if the authority in question is itself a reason for societal problems.

It could be argued that industries that rely on governments and local authorities use local CSR as a strategy. In a developing country context, the outcome may not always "further some social good, beyond the interests of the firm" (McWilliams & Siegel, 2001, p. 117). Energy, mining, transportation and construction companies can be expected, in many cases, to be more responsive to the demands of the relevant authorities than other stakeholders. For future research, Wiig and Kolstad (2010) suggest that this interaction between CSR and institutions in developing country needs further inquiry. Zhao (2012) looked further into business-state relationships in Russia and China, confirming the important role of CSR in this regard. The emerging markets are arguably moving in the direction of increased regulation and pro-active policies; unless this can be said about developing countries, CSR in these locations might require its own theory.

Strike et al. (2006) indirectly confirm the assumption of more and less responsible industries. Their innovative model of CSR and CSiR allows for responsible (CSR) and irresponsible (CSiR) behaviour, capturing two dimensions of industry behaviour at the same time. Upon examining the relevance of industries, they found CSiR higher in the "Mining, Utilities, and Construction" industry (p. 859) whereas the "Food and Other Services" (p. 857) sector stands out with significantly higher CSR performance. The positive role of the food industry is further supported by Aguilera et al. (2007).

Laudal (2010) distinguished industries according to their possible impact on society. The scholar argued that an industry can be characterised by the *CSR potential* it carries, that is "a high potential for positive influence through CSR-related actions" (p. 63). The concept of CSR potential and CSiR might be useful to identify areas where MNEs could make a difference, or where future pressure arises. It does not help to prioritise issues, however.

Upon comparing the rather irresponsible mining industry with the food sector it becomes clear that the latter might be exposed to more pressure, increased competition, and dependence on end consumers. It is therefore imperative for empirical research to consider the industry that is observed. For companies that develop their CSR strategy not only the home and the host country might impact decisions but the industry characteristics in various host countries. In conformity with Sweeney and Coughlan (2008) it can be concluded that industry characteristics imply substantial differences regarding CSR policies. Relevant stakeholders, prominent CSR issues, pressure for standardisation and responsiveness is likely to vary according to the industry-specifics.

4.4.3 Visibility

The visibility of a subsidiary is related to its size (Hamprecht & Schwarzkopf, 2014), aggressive branding (van Tulder & Kolk, 2001), the degree to which it is exposed to a larger range of stakeholders (Rodriguez et al., 2006), in particular the number of customers (Young & Makhija, 2014). A highly visible subsidiary faces greater pressure for CSR. It will be under closer scrutiny, causing concerns about its reputation (Strike et al., 2006).

Visibility is increased by a global branding strategy (Polonsky & Jevons, 2009). Nike and Reebok are a case in point. Their visibility and the global presence made them an easy target for NGOs, media reports and consumer boycotts as opposed to unknown footwear companies (van Tulder and Kolk, 2001). Chiu and Sharfman (2011) add that the risk inherent to a business (e.g., a nuclear power plant operator) increases visibility, while business-to-business marketers (e.g., soft drink producers) avoid consumer pressures by large. The latter is also reflected by the marginal attention paid so far towards CSR in global supply chains (Hsueh, 2014).

Based upon these observations, Young and Makhija (2014) developed a framework that attempts to predict a firms *CSR responsiveness*. CSR responsiveness in this case describes "the combined effects of institutional environment and economic motivations on firms' engagement in CSR activities" (p. 671). Prior to this model it has already been assumed that a regulatory framework is positively related to CSR. This still holds true; however, a larger firm size, as well as a larger number of customers, increases visibility. As a result, CSR responsiveness increases even further. From another perspective, the concept of vulnerability comes into play. The concept resembles the influencing strategies of stakeholders by Frooman (1999). Vulnerability is described by Young and Makhija (2014) as a MNEs "dependence on the goodwill of societal actors" which may "increase or decrease the value gained from legitimacy in their environment" (p. 671).

The concept of visibility requires an industry setting, if tested empirically. Young and Makhija (2014) identified the global apparel industry as being an interesting case to investigate. The industry setting is highly competitive, labour-intensive, standardised and under intense cost pressure. Therefore it had drawn much negative attention over the degrading and often dangerous working conditions that applied even to children. The CSR responsiveness was proven to be significantly linked to the outlined concepts, providing renewed support for the legitimacy-seeking foundation and economic motivation of CSR. Less visible firms were found to be less likely to adopt a CSR policy.

The innovative approach of combining sociological (CSR responsiveness) and economic (shareholder) theories in order to understand CSR is both convincing and promising for future research. It is well-suited to capture the wealth maximisation motivation of firms and the influence of society. Although the authors expect their concept to hold in different industry-settings, this assumption has yet to be verified.

4.4.4 Critical summary

Strategic CSR seems to be influenced by several variables. Distance, industry and visibility in particular have been found to influence the relative importance of CSR to a company. The linkage between distance, LOF, and CSR that has been proposed by Campbell et al. (2012) is logically convincing as it is creative. However, further studies under different circumstances will be required to gain a deeper understanding of this relationship. For example, the influence of national culture (Waldman et al., 2006) as well as the regulatory framework (Lo et al., 2008) could have influenced the observation. If MNEs strategically decrease CSR activities in new markets, it could be argued that the global CSR strategy suits especially those companies that internationalised a long time ago and gained sufficient experience. Otherwise, the global strategy suits MNEs that internationalise only within relatively similar markets – e.g., within the developed world.

Industries seem to vary in the CSR issues they address. First, this indicates that MNEs indeed identify stakeholders and policies strategically. Second, some CSR issues suit the global CSR strategy because they do not involve culture but might be certified (e.g., environmental standards). Industries might thus be linked to global CSR strategies in case they emphasise CSR issues that can become standardised. Industries that rely on governmental support tend to exhibit less commitment to CSR than sectors with a large customer base.

Hence industries seem to be linked to visibility. Industries that interact with private customers are more exposed and more likely to become responsive. Visibility influences CSR commitment. The implication for strategy is interesting: A MNE that operates different subsidiaries is likely to avoid a global approach if the subsidiaries differ in their size, competencies and ultimately their respective visibility.

Hence, by linking impacting variables to CSR strategies new insights may be gained. For example, it is unclear whether Husted and Allen (2006) correctly assumed that global CSR in global MNEs indicates a non-strategic approach to CSR. It is conceivable that certain industries favour both a global CSR and a global product-market strategy. On the other hand, other impacting variables might be found that are even more important.

4.5 Superseding CSR?

Porter and Kramer (2002, 2006, 2011) approached CSR from a strategic perspective. In their writings, the scholars do not emphasise the IB context. However, many examples that illustrate their arguments were taken from subsidiaries in emerging markets. In addition, the scholars do not openly derive their recommendations based on academic literature. In fact, the authors abstain from supporting their suggestions with evidence other than hand-picked examples. These examples, however, are convincing as is the supportive echo their concept received.

4.5.1 Shared value concept

The original idea behind the Shared Value Concept (SVC) is straightforward. Companies gain a competitive advantage if they approach CSR not as "a cost, a constraint, or a charitable deed" (Porter & Kramer, 2006, p. 80) but as a part of their core business strategy. In 2002, when Porter and Kramer first suggested a strategic approach to CSR, most businesses according to their observations distinguished two kinds of expenditure: Either the payment benefited business (corporate expenditure), or it was meant to benefit society (CSR). Combining corporate strategy with goals that benefit society would ultimately lead to "a convergence of interests" (Porter & Kramer, 2002, p. 59).

It is this convergence of interests that provides competitive advantages to a firm. Porter and Kramer (2002) identify four key elements in this area that should be considered when selecting relevant CSR issues: *Factor conditions*, *demand conditions*, *context for strategy and rivalry*, and *related and supporting industries*. These elements imply a local CSR strategy. Managers are recommended to identify the factor conditions that could be improved by tailored CSR policies, such as improvement of the physical infrastructure or the availability of skilled workers. Similarly, demand conditions in a community, especially in developing countries, can be influenced by community support. In addition, the context for strategy and rivalry is improved as companies join initiatives such as transparency international and increase efforts to fight corruption. As a result, competition increases and local institutions become more effective in implementing regulations. Finally, supporting industries refers to the suppliers and related companies that a firm relies on. If local industries were supported, a network could emerge lowering transportation cost and increasing innovations. Thus, the strategic CSR management identifies the areas where its own interests overlap with those of society in general and local stakeholders in particular. Porter and Kramer (2002) recommend this approach to be taken towards every important host country. This local CSR approach is justified convincingly by the substantial differences among countries. Factor and demand conditions, for example, will vary significantly between developed and developing countries, offering vastly different opportunities for CSR.

Expanding the theory of shared value, Porter and Kramer (2006) emphasise the need to treat CSR not different from investments into research and development. For strategic CSR constitutes a long-term investment that pays off only if treated with the same seriousness that is given to other operations. To minimise the risk of investing resources in an unfortunate strategy, the scholars emphasise the need to select and prioritise the CSR issues carefully. The importance of an issue depends both on the shared value it might create and the relative importance to the company's core business. This approach is supported from a marketing-perspective by Polonsky and Jevons (2009) who hypothesised that a consistent, focused and clear CSR program will appeal to stakeholders as opposed to a diffuse positioning that signals uncertainty. Rangan et al. (2015) support this notion, calling for aligning clear-cut CSR initiatives with the companies core business.

Porter and Kramer finalised their shared value concept in 2011. SVC is now defined as "policies and operating practices that enhance the competitiveness of a company while simultaneously advancing the economic and social conditions in the communities in which it operates" (p. 66). The concept promises to supersede CSR in that the latter is mainly reputa-tion-driven. CSR, according to the authors, is characterised by a "limited connection to the business" (p. 76). By contrast, SVC focuses on the core business and engages with the communities. It is this approach that yields competitive advantages for MNEs.

Shared value is created by reinventing products and markets, by redefining parts of the value chain and by creating supportive clusters in proximity to company locations. These recommenda-tions are interrelated since redesigned products, for example, would require less resources or provide additional benefits to communities. Companies embracing these opportunities are likely to gradually discover multiple areas where different business units may redesign their operations. As a result, both the company and its stakeholders benefit (Porter & Kramer, 2011).

From a society-perspective, both NGOs and governments are encouraged to use regulations in a way that stipulate shared value instead of hampering businesses by ill-designed bureaucratic regulations. As long as MNEs are perceived as a threat rather than an opportunity, both society and business will forgo valuable opportunities for joining forces in the fight for sustainable development. For example, prices for resources have to reflect their true cost and may thus be regulated. On the other hand, if a performance standard is introduced it should be left to the company to meet this standard. Market mechanism and stakeholder regulations are able to enforce change much quicker and substantial than enforced over regulation.

This is an important aspect often overlooked. Traditional CSR theories support a positive relationship between the regulatory and institutional environment of a country and CSR (e.g., Lo et al., 2008; Yang & Rivers, 2009; Zhao et al., 2014), yet they rarely offer advise to governments and civil society nor do they differentiate between supportive and counterproductive regulation. On the other hand, if looked at from a strategic perspective, it remains questionable to what degree MNEs from different industries will embrace this aspect of shared value if adopted by governments.

4.5.2 Contesting shared value

Crane, Palazzo, Spence, and Matten (2014) are the first renowned academics to offer an extended critique of the shared value concept. Managers, the media and even researchers, they admit, have welcomed the concept enthusiastically especially in light of the financial crisis. Refining capitalism by turning conflicting goals of business and society into an opportunities, Crane et al. (2014) acknowledge, is a very tempting offer. However, the scholars maintain that it lacks originality, ignores the fundamental tension between business and society and fails to justify its optimism about the promised alignment of corporate and societal goals.

Crane et al. (2014) object the originality of shared value because it is deeply rooted in stakeholder theory, strategic CSR and several related concepts that have been developed recently. Most prominent among them is the concept of blended value, social innovation, local capacity and native capability (e.g., Crane et al., 2014; London & Hart, 2004; Simola, 2007). It supersedes, the critics stress, CSR only in as far as "they construct a largely unrecognisable caricature of CSR that they can dismiss" (p. 134).

What is more, tension between business and society are not solved but rather ignored. In many cases, managers face different stakeholders with opposing goals. Suppliers demand higher returns while employees expect increased wages. In other cases, becoming more responsible has no or negative affects on profitability. This is not taken into account when Porter and Kramer (2011) expect a company to prioritise their CSR issues from a business perspective only. In Porter's diamond model, for example, market attractiveness is determined by the bargaining power of suppliers and customers. If suppliers, Crane at al. (2014) note, were empowered as proposed by the shared value concept, their bargaining power would increase. This would weaken the position of the company, at least under free competition.

What is more, the careful selection of prioritised CSR issues may convince managers to invest only in convenient problems instead of accepting the full range of challenges that businesses face. Ignoring an important problem by adopting a SVC approach does not benefit society. Thus, the scholars do not deny that encouraging examples of successful shared value projects exist. They warn, however, that a dismissal of CSR and adoption of shared value strategies could lead to "islands of win-win projects in an ocean of unsolved environmental and social conflicts" (p. 139). To refute this claim, Porter, Kramer, and researchers in general would have to conduct cross-country and cross-industry studies on MNEs adopting the approach. In fact, based on the observation by Strike et al. (2006) it could be assumed that SVC creates and destroys value. Strike et al. (2006) found that companies became both more responsible and irresponsible after internationalising, a fact that might be explained by increased opportunities and challenges. If SVC was to be superior to strategic CSR, a study comparing MNEs that use either approach would clarify these problems.

4.5.3 The bottom of the pyramid

While these arguments cast doubt on the promise of Porter and Kramer to supersede CSR, especially strategic CSR, their shared value concept may be viewed as an important contribution to the local CSR strategy. Much of their attention has been focused on examples of successful community involvement in developing countries. The majority of citizens in these countries constitute the so called *bottom of the pyramid* (BOP). The term refers to a market that encompasses four billion people. They are the poorest, yet largest socio-economic category today, living on $2/day or even less (Prahalad, 2012). The potential of this market has long been overlooked and requires distinct strategies, one of which could be derived from the shared value concept.

Arnold and Valentin (2013) differentiate between profitability and empowerment. MNEs that enter these markets may operate profitable, yet the poverty of their customers and employees makes them vulnerable since they lack any form of bargaining power. Empowerment, on the other hand, is a goal often pursued by NGOs and the United Nations. MNEs that combine profitability with empowerment gain in numerous ways. Possible partnerships with renowned institutions and the reputation gained aside, these responsible MNEs nurture loyal stakeholders, empower new customers and possible employees, and create new markets.

London and Hart (2004) noted quite early that successful MNE subsidiaries catering to BOP customers need to pay special attention to non-traditional local partners including non-profit organisations, village elderlies and community groups. These local partners provide the subsidiary with valuable information, resources and the required legitimacy, which in turn provided them with suitable products, employment opportunities and investments. London and Hart (2004) emphasise that not only local responsiveness but *local capacity building* was required to operate successful, that is "the sharing of resources outside firm boundaries" (p. 363). The notion of sharing resources is strikingly similar to the process described in more detail by Porter and Kramer (2006).

The distinct characteristics of BOP markets seem to require another form of CSR than developed markets or even the wealthier consumers emerging markets. As noticed by Jain and De Moya (2013) in the Indian context, no MNE website displayed content on CSR in the local language. The authors explain this by the fact that people targeted by CSR information will belong to the more privileged classes that prefer English content. CSR that relates to poor communities might be communicated to other stakeholders, yet in order to be successful, its content and orientation has to be distinct. The emphasis of this strategy is collaboration with and empowerment of communities that often lack basic needs.

To this end, London and Hart (2004) emphasise the need to overcome a mere adaptation of global CSR policies. In one case, a subsidiary had a high CSR reputation at home that focused on donations to third parties. In the BOP context no changes were made – a perfect example of a global CSR strategy and the type of CSR that has been rejected so strongly by Porter and Kramer (2002). Instead, London and Hart (2004) explain, CSR should aim at "identifying and strengthening business-critical existing institutions in the local market environment" (p. 364).

In another environment, publicity about donations and charity may enhance a brand image. The BOP market, however, requires a vastly different understanding. The CSR policy that meets these distinct needs has to be very responsive, even to differences within larger countries such as India (Prahalad, 2012). Not only are the markets distinct from developing countries, large differences exist among various BOP markets. In Brazil, the majority of poor people live in overcrowded cities, while in Bangladesh most people live in isolated villages in the countryside (Arnold & Valentin, 2013).

MNE subsidiaries that attempt to cater to the BOP, according to London and Hart (2004), will have to develop a *local capability* based on a variety of partners, tailored solutions and a bottom-up approach that emphasises innovation in a developmental sense. Hence, the concept of shared value might contribute to a CSR concept that serves as a BOP-market strategy. This assessment is supported by the Rangan, Chase, and Karim (2015) who found most managers to embrace the idea of shared value, yet the majority of them failed to transform the idea into a strategy. A possible solution to this problem could be a distinction between developed country CSR and BOP markets.

5 Discussion: Implications for strategy

Barin Cruz and Boehe noted in 2010 that neither managerial and nor academic literature offered a comprehensive overview of MNE strategies concerning CSR. As it has been shown this is about to change. The present discussion attempts to derive and evaluate the key findings of the present study. This may contribute towards a unifying framework for international strategic CSR.

Three major findings of the present discussion are very clear already. From a managerial perspective it has been shown that MNEs engage in CSR policies worldwide. The challenge for subsidiaries is to balance pressures for integration and responsiveness strategically. From an academic perspective the surge in studies on international strategic CSR is evident. The challenge for researchers is to twofold: Empirical studies are limited because of a lack of data sources and the difficulties involved in gathering these data independently. Theoretical studies cope with the lack of commonly accepted definitions and the variety of concepts, assumptions and related theories.

Last but not least, many questions remain to be answered by further research. Building on the discussion of the implications from an academic perspective, some suggestions were made in this regard. CSR increasingly becomes an integral part of business strategies. The theoretical framework that serves as a linkage between the evolving literatures has yet to be created.

5.1 Implications for management

Managers are well advised to consider the strategic options offered by CSR policies. CSR is a long-term investment that ought to be intertwined with the company's core business (Porter & Kramer, 2006). It has been proposed to use the PESTEL framework to develop or decompose CSR strategies of MNEs (Lu et al., 2014). This framework examines the political, economic, social, technological, ecological and legal environment that impacts on the corporation. Based on the reviewed literature, a slightly different approach is suggested. Creating a CSR strategy ideally involves three distinct steps: The *business perspective*, the *societal perspective*, and the *organisational perspective*.

5.1.1 The business perspective

The business perspective considers the resources and competencies of the firm as described by Porter and Kramer (2006, 2011). The competitive context, the industry and the visibility of the company influences the degree to which CSR becomes vital for the company's success (Laudal, 2011; Young & Makhija, 2014). Competitors which adopt certified standards make it imperative for the MNE to follow soon, for absence would be interpreted by stakeholders as irresponsible and reactive at best (Muller, 2006). High competition and high visibility increase the need for consistent CSR in general, while different industries vary in the degree to which they emphasise individual CSR issues (Sweeney & Coughlan, 2008). CSR potential denotes the impact that CSR initiatives have in a given industry (Laudal, 2010). The business perspective aims at identifying necessary and potential CSR policies and the degree to which CSR is vital for a MNE.

5.1.2 The societal perspective

The societal perspective is equally important. Long-term investments cannot be made in a reactive manner. The strategy ought to be based on a profound understanding of the stakeholder groups. Managing stakeholder relations involves three steps: First, identifying salient stakeholder groups (Frooman, 1999). Second, identifying the CSR issue which might influence relations with this stakeholder positively (Reimann et al., 2012). Third, understanding the underlying expectations and values as they might be changing over time.

This is especially true in two relatively new markets: Emerging markets that increase regulations and witness an empowered civil society, and BOP markets that demand shared value initiatives. Ignoring changing demands in emerging markets leads to legitimacy crises (Zhao et al., 2014), while traditional CSR policies in BOP markets lead to failure (London & Hart, 2004; Prahalad, 2012). A MNE should therefore identify not simply geographic or cultural regions but market segments it is catering for. This approach ensures understanding of stakeholders and building lasting relationships that ensure mutual benefits.

Once the relevant stakeholders and major CSR issues are identified, a marketing approach might be useful to design them in a way which appeals to respective addressees (Bhattacharya et al., 2009). The relevant CSR subjects should be consistent (Oikonomou et al., 2014) and focused (Polonsky & Jevons, 2009) and often depend on the respective industry a MNE is operating in (Muller, 2006; Sweeney & Coughlan, 2008)

When designing CSR policies it is likewise important to understand the concept of the logic dilemma. Comprehending the cultures and ethics of the host countries is not sufficient, for one logic would have to accept the dominance of the other (Tan & Wang, 2011). Hypernorms may provide ethical guidelines for managers in cross-cultural environments (Donaldson & Dunfee, 1999), yet the core values which are inherent to different cultures cannot apply simultaneously. In addition, the cultural background of a subsidiary manager may impact the level of his CSR commitment as long as vision and leadership is absent (Waldman et al., 2006). Ingraining CSR into corporate culture may contribute to ensure commitment across affiliates (Barin Cruz & Pedrozo, 2009; Barin Cruz & Boehe, 2010).

5.1.3 The organisational perspective

All these considerations have an impact on the organisational perspective. Depending on the size of the MNE and the differences among the host countries, each subsidiary will develop its individual assessment. Upon reviewing the results of the business and societal perspective, an organisational strategy will be required, which determines the way CSR policies are designed and implemented. According to the literature reviewed, three major options exist: The *global*, *local*, and *transnational* strategy. To determine the suitable strategy, not only pressures have to be considered but the feasibility and complexity associated with the respective strategy.

The *global strategy* is consistent and efficient. Its popularity is enhanced by certified standards and an international harmonisation of CSR. Environmental issues and basic human rights were among the issues that are often considered global (Husted and Allen, 2006). The global strategy might require less control from the head quarter (Muller, 2006). On top of this it has been observed that CSR increasingly absorbs Asian and non-American ideas (Waddock, 2008). As stakeholder demands and CSR concepts converge, the idea of universal policies and ethics may gain popularity and foster global CSR policies.

The *local strategy* ensures the policy is suitable and more efficacious than a standardised one. A MNE which operates in very different countries is likely to localise its CSR strategy. Without considering the idiosyncrasies of a given market it becomes much more difficult to gain a competitive advantage build on CSR (Park et al., 2014). In fact, a range of literature criticises the lack of responsiveness shown by developed-country based MNEs in emerging markets (e.g., Bondy & Starkey, 2014; Jain & De Moya, 2013; Jamali, 2010). Similarly, however, it has been recognised that local CSR forgoes an organisational learning process (Barin Cruz & Boehe, 2010) and might be perceived as ad-hoc approach and reactive (Muller, 2006).

The *transnational strategy* is sometimes considered to be the most appropriate approach to CSR for reaping the benefits of integration and responsiveness (Stahl & Sully de Luque, 2014). Literature suggests three ways to achieve this aim. The basic version of transnational CSR distinguishes between a centralised decision making process and a local implementation process that allows for adaptation (Bondy & Starkey, 2014). Organisational learning may enhance the CSR program by informing the head quarter about challenges and opportunities encountered in the host countries (Logsdon & Wood, 2002, 2005).

The second suggestion distinguishes between global and local issues (Husted & Allen, 2006). A MNE identifies a limited number of global CSR issues and subsidiaries decide to add local CSR initiatives, based on their capability, size and stakeholder pressure. A subsidiary that is highly depended on external stakeholders is likely to become more responsive (Hah & Freeman, 2014).

The most complex strategy is transverse CSR management. This approach involves not only the global and local management, but ingrains CSR into the core business, comprises different business units and diffuses into the company culture (Barin Cruz & Boehe, 2010). This strategy was observed in the retail industry that is known for its above average CSR performance (Aguilera et al., 2007). The organisational learning, the communication processes within the head quarter and subsidiaries, and the company culture are likely to provide lasting advantages to a MNE that applies this strategy. Managers should ensure the feasibility and the existence of sufficient resources, though. It could be argued the size of a company, the degree of internationalisation and the competitive context influence the urgency of this strategy.

5.2 Implications for research

International strategic CSR is an innovative field of research that increasingly gains momentum. However, being an evolving subject the limitations, research gaps, and challenges that remain should not be overlooked. Three major challenges can be identified based on the present literature review: First, the lack of conceptual clarity, or *prevailing inconsistencies*; second, the scarcity of data bases and the seemingly unrelated *empirical studies*; and third, the need for *theoretical frameworks* that include findings and contribute towards a more coherent approach towards CSR.

5.2.1 Inconsistency

Inconsistencies are fertilising the debate and might be considered a common phenomenon in the context of an evolving concept. However, as the number of studies increases, the need for clarity becomes more pressing. Clarity is needed with regards to definitions, concepts and observed patterns.

This study noted in the beginning that CSR lacks a final, commonly accepted definition. This problem has been solved in three ways: Numerous authors refer to either the definition of McWilliams and Siegel (2001) or Carroll (1979) (e.g., Christmann & Taylor, 2006; Reimann et al., 2012; Waldman et al., 2006; Yang & Rivers, 2009). Others maintain no final definition would be necessary since the term denotes the complex and changing relationship between businesses and societies (e.g., Matten & Moon, 2008; Palazzo & Scherer, 2006; Snider et al., 2003). Again, a third tendency emphasises a particular aspect of CSR or closely related concepts. Examples range from *green management* (Barin Cruz & Pedrozo, 2009) to *climate change* (Hamprecht & Schwarzkopf, 2014) and *business ethics* (Doh et al, 2010; Kolk & van Tulder, 2004; Tan & Wang, 2011).

While a variety of definitions might be appreciated as enriching the debate (Arthaud-Day, 2005), there is a persisting tendency to coin even new terms which could be described as sub-groups or equivalents of CSR. These terms range from *corporate responsibility* (CR) (Egri & Ralston, 2008) to *corporate social strategy* (CSS) (Husted & Allen, 2007) to *corporate environmental responsibility* (CER) (Dögl & Holtbrügge, 2014). This makes it difficult for researchers to gather the relevant literature and to compare the major findings.

This observation holds true in the case of global, local and transnational CSR as well. Definitions have been proposed quite early by Logsdon and Wood (2005) and Arthaud-Day (2005). Both scholars are mentioned by Husted and Allen (2006), however the latter argue no theory would exist on global and local CSR. Hence their definition frames CSR in a slightly different way. Logsdon and Wood (2005) understand global CSR to be centrally managed. Similarly, Arthaud-Day (2005) relates the concept to global codes and a centralised structure. Husted and Allen (2006) distinguish between global and local CSR on the basis of "the community that demands it" (p. 840). This is problematic because describing certain *CSR issues* as global (e.g., human rights) and others as local (e.g., unemployment) seems quite arbitrarily. The authors argue that universal standards will be demanded everywhere, while local problems differ among countries. However, it could be argued unemployment is a problem which arises in most if not all societies, whereas specific human rights are influenced by values of different societies. Issues might therefore be considered global by one author and local by another. What is more, this definition does not explain whether the CSR strategy has been developed at the head quarter or the subsidiary. CSR that addresses employees might have been developed centrally as well as locally.

Muller (2006) defines the global CSR strategy as an adaptation of home country CSR practises by the subsidiaries. This definition allows for a decentralised structure since the subsidiary might choose independently to adopt the global strategy, yet the underlying assumption resembles the definition of Logsdon and Wood (2005). Jamali (2010) as well as Jain and De Moya (2013) combined the definitions of Husted and Allen (2006) and Muller (2006) with an emphasis on the advantages and disadvantages of the global and local CSR strategy.

Clarity is needed with regards to several other concepts as well. Transnational CSR has been termed "hybrid" (Logsdon & Wood, 2002), "integrated" (Bondy & Starkey, 2014), "glocal" (Jain & De Moya, 2013), and "diluted" (Jamali, 2010) CSR. The concept of *CSR ingrainedness* seems to be equivalent to *CSR reputation*. CSR ingrainedness refers to "degree to which a corporation prioritizes CSR in its strategy and systematically and routinely incorporates CSR into its daily practices" (Tan & Wang, 2011, p. 378), while CSR reputation refers to "a firm known for its concern for social or environmental issues" (Campbell et al., 2012, p. 91). The third category of inconsistencies concerns the interpretation of empirical observations.

5.2.2 Empirical studies

Empirical studies have to choose the perspective which is taken, as well as the data that is used. Furthermore, the present state of the art should be taken into consideration in order to move beyond the initial debate.

Perspectives on MNEs might be related to the strategy that is examined. One approach examines head quarter perspectives (Bondy & Starkey, 2014) while another approach takes the perspective of subsidiaries (e.g., Husted & Allen, 2006; Muller, 2006). The former is useful to understand organisational aspects of CSR, especially in case a transnational strategy is pursued. The latter allows to compare a set of subsidiaries in one host country. Since subsidiaries face similar opportunities and challenges in this environment their respective strategies can be compared. In case both head quarter and subsidiary perspectives were taken, the number of MNEs became very limited (Barin Cruz & Pedrozo, 2009; Barin Cruz &

Boehe, 2010; Hamprecht & Schwarzkopf, 2014). Very few studies have taken this approach so far although insights might be very interesting.

The largest obstacle towards empirical research is the scarcity of data (Husted & Allen, 2006; Strike et al., 2006). Scholars coping with this problem mostly resort to interviews with managers (Barin Cruz & Pedrozo, 2009; Bondy & Starkey, 2014; Jamali, 2010), company websites (Jain & De Moya, 2013) or the KLD and Co. Index that evaluates CSR performance of US-based MNEs (Campbell et al., 2012; Chiu & Sharfman, 2011; Strike et al., 2006). Reliable data bases not only allow for efficient data collection but also ensure a degree of objectivity that might be lost during interviews and websites. As suggested by Kolk and van Tulder (2010), building a large-scale database could accelerate and enhance understanding of CSR strategies tremendously.

In order to improve the state of the art it is decisive to link new papers to the growing body of existing literature. Hamprecht and Schwarzkopf (2014), for example, observed a MNE that exhibited a low CSR ingrainedness and subsidiaries that encountered high ethical pressure. The theoretical framework of Tan and Wang (2011) is able to explain the subsequent CSR initiatives by the subsidiary, which the authors termed *compliance strategy*. Yet Hamprecht and Schwarzkopf (2014) do not refer to Tan and Wang; instead, they introduce a new concept (institutional trinity).

Sometimes, misunderstandings can be observed as well. Bondy and Starkey (2014), for example, assume that Husted and Allen (2006) ignored the transnational approach. The scholars defined *CSR issues* as being either global or local, which should be taken into question. However, they actually did allow for simultaneous adoption of global and local CSR issues – a strategy that would be transnational, according to their own definition.

Having said this, several recent empirical papers indicate increasing reference to earlier studies. This is true especially for Bondy and Starkey (2014), Jain and De Moya (2013) and Jamali (2010). Future empirical research should evolve around two major challenges: First, testing theoretical frameworks that need empirical verification. Second, testing present empirical findings under different circumstances. Suggestions will be outlined in more detail in the sub-chapter on future research.

5.2.3 Theoretical frameworks

Egri and Ralston (2008) found that only one quarter of international CSR literature is of a theoretical nature. The major theoretical contributions to strategic CSR have been derived from stakeholder theory (Freeman, 1984) and institutional theory (Kostova & Roth, 2002; Kostova & Zaheer, 1999). Recently it has been suggested to include political behaviour literature (Jamali, 2010), CAGE distance and LOF (Campbell et al., 2012), as well as national culture (Waldman et al., 2006), hypernorms (Arthaud-Day, 2005; Logsdon & Wood, 2005), and core values (Tan & Wang, 2011).

As noted by Hah and Freeman (2014), the challenge is yet to consolidate and combine the present theories. Based on the reviewed literature, three consolidations can be suggested: Unifying the transnational strategy framework, conceptualising the transverse management, and integrating the aspects that relate to culture.

The transnational solution was described by Husted and Allen (2006) as simultaneous consideration of global and local CSR issues in a subsidiary. Jamali (2010) proposed that distinct subsidiaries would differ in the degree to which they engage in global and local CSR. Transnational CSR in this case could denote the tendency of a given subsidiary towards a more standardised/responsive approach to CSR. Hah and Freeman (2014) advanced this idea in their well-conceived conceptual framework. The framework combines important contributions by Yang and Rivers (2009), Jamali (2010), as well as Tan and Wang (2011).

Since the perspective of a subsidiary is taken, the network structure of MNEs might be captured in a more realistic sense. A decision by the head quarter to either pursue a fully standardised or decentralised CSR strategy in all subsidiaries might be unrealistic in many cases. Young and Makhija (2014) contributed in this regard by introducing the concepts of visibility and vulnerability of individual subsidiaries. Park and Ghauri (2015) distinguish large and small or medium sized subsidiaries of MNEs, emphasising the lack of attention towards CSR strategies of the latter. The impacting variables distance, industry, and visibility in general may contribute to a deeper understanding of subsidiary behaviour. Similarly interesting is that the conceptual framework addresses the concern expressed by Bondy and Starkey (2014) who questioned the feasibility of a purely transnational CSR. The most important limitation of the conceptual framework is probably the lack of a designation – contrary to the creativity observed in most papers.

The transverse management (Barin Cruz & Pedrozo, 2009; Barin Cruz & Boehe, 2010) can be viewed as an extension of the global business citizenship model (Logsdon & Wood, 2002, 2005). Again, the major difficulty is associated mainly with differing terminology and the missing reference towards the work of Logsdon and Wood. The model has to be tested among varying industries and countries, and a combination with the shared value concept might be useful. Ingraining CSR into corporate culture, integrating different business units and linking CSR to the corporations' core business definitely is a very promising notion.

Culture and ethics is the least connected subject in international CSR. Hypernorms guide ethics, yet Tan and Wang (2011) convincingly assume that core values are likely to conflict among different cultures. The notion of arising universal values interestingly goes back to the beginning of the last decade; there might be a reason why recent studies increasingly emphasise responsiveness over universalism. Expectations towards companies increase in emerging markets and may converge with those held in developed countries; yet few developments indicate a convergence of culture, values and beliefs.

While hypernorms and core values describe conflicts that may arise in host countries, national culture and global leadership is concerned with managerial values and decision-making. While this stream of literature is out of scope, strategic CSR frameworks could account for the influence of managerial values, corporate culture, and host country culture. Then, in turn, might this aspect be combined with the findings of Tan and Wang (2011).

The major implications for theoretical frameworks are therefore twofold: First, empirically testing and subsequently consolidating the considerable developments in international strategic CSR theories. Second, creative linkages between existing concepts in IB literature and CSR may provide useful insights. Distance and LOF are good examples in this regard. Cross-fertilising insights from different fields of research can be expected to increase with regards to international CSR strategies (Doh et al., 2010; Jamali, 2010).

5.3 Limitations and future research

The present study attempted to include the diverse and evolving literature that contributes to international CSR strategies. Recurring searches, a wide range of key words, as well as the inclusion of articles referred to all minimised the risk of overlooking important literature. The inconsistent terminology indicates that some articles might have been missed, however.

A wide range of literature contributes towards international CSR by examining country-specific cases. The emphasis on MNEs as well as the strategy perspective marginalised findings of these papers. Future papers may thus examine CSR in emerging markets (e.g., Meyer, 2004; Muller & Kolk, 2009) or bottom of the pyramid markets (Arnold & Valentin, 2013; London & Hart, 2004). Similarly, specific regions (e.g., Latin America, South East Asia) and countries (e.g., China) may yield relevant insights not only for responsiveness but changing expectations of stakeholders (e.g., Chapple & Moon, 2007; Park, & Zhou, 2014; Zhao, 2012; Zhao et al., 2014). Traditional CSR literature has been developed with a focus on the industrialised world, thereby limiting its usability for an international business context (Egri & Ralston, 2008; Muller & Kolk, 2009). Thus, examining CSR in specific environments may facilitate an understanding of similarities and differences across cultures, regions and countries.

Another promising stream of literature investigates CSR in the supply chain of MNEs. Visibility of MNEs has been found to correspond with increased CSR (Young & Makhija, 2014). Supply chains and global value chains are invisible in most cases, yet a considerable share of wealth creation happens to be associated with suppliers. Practises harmful to the environment, poor working conditions, and resulting scandals within supply chains may affect the MNE as well. An evolving stream of literature contributes towards responsible supply chain management (e.g., Barin Cruz & Boehe, 2008; Hsueh, 2014; Harwood & Humby, 2008). Since supply chain management is outside the scope of the paper, these findings have not been included.

5.3.1 Limitations of strategic CSR

International CSR strategies carry some inherent limitations that apply to most of the papers reviewed. As it has been discussed earlier, researchers encountered numerous difficulties when gathering reliable data. In addition, empirical studies often assume that companies either do have a strategy for CSR (e.g., Jain & De Moya, 2013) or forgo strategic opportunities offered by CSR (e.g., Jamali, 2010). As suggested recently by Rangan et al. (2015), this assumption might be misleading. The authors found CSR programs to be uncoordinated in many instances, with no CEO involvement and little concern for long-term strategies. Having a CSR program does not always imply an underlying strategic logic (Porter & Kramer, 2002; London & Hart, 2004). This does in no way change the potential of CSR to gain competitive advantages. However, it does emphasise that not all empirical findings necessarily covered an actively, well-conceived strategy. Only a unified and verified CSR theory will be able to convincingly detect cases that clearly involved little strategic planning since the present range of impacting variables is too large.

Theoretical frameworks are often limited by their inability to grasp the influence of CSR on business operations. Examples include the ongoing debate on the relationship between CSR and financial performance (e.g., Barnett, 2007; Lu et al., 2014) and the relationship between improved working conditions and employee performance (Reimann et al., 2012). The transverse CSR management structure involves substantial resource commitments of the MNE. So far strategic CSR literature struggles to provide the tools for a more precise cost-benefit analysis which helps managers to understand the strategic options at their disposal.

5.3.2 Future research questions

Three major fields might be considered for future research. The empirical verification of theoretical frameworks, the empirical testing of exploratory studies, and the combination of insights from recent studies into new research questions.

None of the theoretical frameworks covered in this literature review has been taken as the foundation of an empirical investigation. The theoretical framework presented by Arthaud-Day (2005), for example, has not systematically been taken as a framework for empirical research. Even the aspect that gained attention – the introduction of the global, multinational, and transnational MNE and the related CSR strategy – has only been tested on a country-bases. Similarly, the theoretical contributions by Yang and Rivers (2009) as well as Tan and Wang (2011) have not been tested to date. Yet the probably most important testing regards the conceptual framework developed by Hah and Freeman (2014). This might be difficult due to the variety of corporate and societal impacting variables as well as the scarcity of data on subsidiary CSR programs. However, if a future framework was to be created for international CSR strategies, than these observations could significantly enhance and improve its theoretical underpinnings.

Many present studies were of an exploratory nature. To understand their implications, additional research could test the hypotheses under new circumstances. For example, Muller (2006) found subsidiary autonomy to be related to higher CSR performance. This observation involved European headquarters, subsidiaries in Mexico and MNEs from the automotive industry. As discussed earlier, researchers should be aware of industry influences (e.g., Sweeney & Coughlan, 2008) and substantial differences between developed countries, emerging markets and BOP markets (e.g., London & Hart, 2004; Robertson, 2009; van Tulder & Kolk, 2001; Zhao et al., 2014).

In this vein, it would be interesting to overcome the limitations of the study by Campbell et al. (2012). CAGE distance and LOF was tested for US-based MNEs from the financial sector. Future research could inquire the influence of CAGE distances on CSR between different industries. Similarly interesting would be a sample of emerging-country based MNEs. Different industries may reveal different patterns that depend on their visibility (Young & Makhija, 2014). The emerging market based MNEs require more research regarding their CSR policies in general (Egri & Ralston, 2008). In this particular setting it might be assumed that LOF for Chinese or Indian MNEs which enter industrialised countries is particularly high. In addition, the regulative framework in the European Union would demand an increase in CSR compared to the MNEs domestic markets. Thus, the CAGE distance could positively correlate to CSR. Simultaneously, this study could provide evidence for the compliance strategy proposed by Tan and Wang (2011).

Finally, combining recent insights into new research questions will undoubtedly yield similarly important results for international CSR strategies. One important aspect regards the relationship between specific CSR issues and individual stakeholder groups. Reimann et al. (2012) presented very robust evidence for related and unrelated linkages in their cross-industry and cross-country study. According to this paper, a specific CSR initiative (e.g., improving working conditions) does influence a particular stakeholder group (e.g., employees increase their working performance), while others remain indifferent towards the policy (e.g., local authorities do not review their relationship to the company after working conditions have been improved). As noted by Jamali (2010), subsidiaries often have no mechanism to measure the impact of their CSR activities on stakeholder groups. Strategic CSR management requires an understanding of these cause and effect relations, however. This is supported by Lu et al. (2014) who tested the relationship between specific aspects of CSR and financial performance. Similar papers examine relations to local authorities in emerging markets (Reimann et al., 2012; Zhao, 2012), environmental CSR (Dögl & Holtbrügge, 2014; Hamprecht & Schwarzkopf, 2014), and the ISO 9000 certificate (Christmann & Taylor, 2006) with regards to international CSR strategies.

Another interesting field of research regards the role of a subsidiary network. It has been noted that empirical research involves a head quarter, subsidiary or holistic perspective. As noted by Bondy and Starkey (2014), the most pressing research gap regards transnational CSR strategies. Studies addressing this gap could be conducted according to the work of Barin Cruz and Boehe (2010), expanding the scope of interest to different industries and countries. However, building on the definition of MNEs as networks (Cavusgil et al., 2012) and following Jamali (2010) in her observation of subsidiary networks, another approach is equally conceivable. Different subsidiaries of the same MNE could be compared in terms of their functions, capabilities, subsidiary size, market size, and dependency on the head quarter (Hah & Freeman, 2014). The observations may indicate that the ideal type of either global or local CSR is much less common than indicated by most studies. If the degree of commitment to CSR and the degree of responsiveness correlates with the subsidiary size and related variables, the conceptual framework by Hah & Freeman (2014) might serve as an alternative to the complex transverse strategy – at least for those MNEs that struggle with such an approach. Testing and further developing this conceptual framework should lie at the centre of researchers' attention in the foreseeable future.

6 Conclusion

MNEs around the world increasingly adopt CSR policies. CSR holds the potential to provide these MNEs with competitive advantages if managed strategically. Strategy in international business aims first and foremost at balancing pressures for integration and responsiveness.

Based on empirical findings and theoretical frameworks, the global, local and transnational CSR strategy was examined. A global CSR strategy builds on standardisation and global leadership. While being consistent and efficient, it might be inappropriate and forgo the advantages of local CSR. The local strategy builds on institutional and stakeholder pressure arising from the host country. Responsiveness provides the company with legitimacy, while CSR policies will be suitable and effective. Again, the disadvantages of this approach do not only regard inconsistencies but the hazard of exploiting lower standards abroad.

Transnational CSR carries the potential to overcome the limitations of the global and local perspective, yet this strategy is more difficult to adopt. Recent literature suggests two approaches to the transnational strategy. The conceptual framework builds on the network character of the MNE. Different subsidiaries of a MNE vary in the degree to which they adopt a global or local strategy, based on internal and external pressures. The other approach suggests a transverse CSR management that ingrains CSR into business units and the corporate culture. The MNE leverages local experiences globally by means of organisational learning.

Impacting variables influence CSR as they influence strategy. Taking the important variables of distance, industry and visibility, it has been shown that not one strategy fits for every MNE. Similarly, research findings are often influenced by the limitations these variables impose. By recognising this relationship, future research may yield interesting results that support managerial decisions and specify antecedents and outcomes of specific configurations.

The SVC finally promised to supersede CSR. The concept is valuable for it emphasises the potential of strategically managed CSR. However, critics maintained rightly that this approach lacks originality. The BOP market was found to have distinct characteristics which could be addressed by the SVC concept. As do distance, industry and visibility impact on the MNE strategy, so do the characteristics of its market. While this implies increased pressure for responsiveness, the growth in certified standards increases pressure towards standardisation.

The final answer on how to manage international CSR strategically ultimately depends on the individual MNE. Based on the literature review, most subsidiaries will tend to adopt a more or less responsive approach depending on internal and external pressure, while those corporations that succeed in adopting the transverse CSR management could gain the most substantial advantages.

7 Abbreviations

BOP	Bottom of the Pyramid
CAGE	Cultural, administrative, geographic, economic (distance)
CER	Corporate Environmental Responsibility
CSR	Corporate Social Responsibility
ISO	International Organization for Standardization
JIBS	Journal of International Business Studies
KLD & Co.	Kinder, Lydenberg, Domini and Company (index)
LOF	Liability of foreignness
MNC	Multinational Corporation, see also: MNE
MNE	Multinational Enterprise
NGO	Non-governmental organisation
OECD	Organisation for Economic Co-operation and Development
PESTEL	Political, economic, social, technological, ecological and legal (factors)
SVC	Shared Value Concept
UN	United Nations
WOS	Web of Science

8 References

Aguilera, R. V., Rupp, D. E., Williams, C. A., & Ganapathi, J. (2007). Putting the S back in corporate social responsibility: A multilevel theory of social change in organizations. *Academy of Management Review, 32*(3), 836–863. doi:10.5465/amr.2007.25275678

Arnold, D. G., & Valentin, A. (2013). Corporate social responsibility at the base of the pyramid. *Journal of Business Research, 66*(10), 1904–1914. doi:10.1016/j.jbusres.2013.02.012

Arthaud–Day, M. L. (2005). Transnational corporate social repsonsibility: A tri–dimensional approach to international CSR research. *Business Ethics Quarterly, 15*(1), 1–22. doi:10.5840/beq20051515

Barin Cruz, L., & Boehe, D. M. (2008). CSR in the global marketplace: Towards sustainable global value chains. *Management Decision, 46*(8), 1187–1209. doi:10.1108/'00251740810901381

Barin Cruz, L., & Boehe, D. M. (2010). How do leading retail MNCs leverage CSR globally? Insights from Brazil. *Journal of Business Ethics, 91*(2), 243–263. doi:10.1007/s10551-010-0617-8

Barin Cruz, L., & Pedrozo, E. A. (2009). Corporate social responsibility and green management: Relation between headquarters and subsidiary in multinational corporations. *Management Decision, 47*(7), 1174–1199. doi:10.1108/00251740910978368

Barnett, M. L. (2007). Stakeholder influence capacity and the variability of financial returns to corporate social responsibility. *Academy of Management Review, 32*(3), 794–816. doi:10.5465/AMR.2007.25275520

Bartlett, C. A., & Ghoshal, S. (1998). *Managing across borders: The transnational solution* (2nd ed.). Boston, MA: Harvard Business School Press.

Bhattacharya, C. B., Korschun, D., & Sen, S. (2009). Strengthening stakeholder–company relationships through mutually beneficial corporate social responsibility initiatives. *Journal of Business Ethics, 85*(S2), 257–272. doi:10.1007/s10551-008-9730-3

Bondy, K., & Starkey, K. (2014). The dilemmas of internationalization: Corporate social responsibility in the multinational corporation. *British Journal of Management, 25*(1), 4–22. doi:10.1111/j.1467-8551.2012.00840.x

Bosch–Badia, M., Montllor–Serrats, J., & Tarrazon, M. (2013). Corporate social responsibility from Friedman to Porter and Kramer. *Theoretical Economics Letters, 3*(3A), 11–15. doi:10.4236/tel.2013.33A003

Bowen, H. R. (1953). *Social responsibilities of the businessman.* New York, NY: Harper & Row.

Campbell, J. L. (2007). Why would corporations behave in socially responsible ways? An institutional theory of corporate social responsibility. *Academy of Management Review, 32*(3): 946–967. doi:10.5465/AMR.2007.25275684

Campbell, J. T., Eden, L., & Miller, S. R. (2012). Multinationals and corporate social responsibility in host countries: Does distance matter? *Journal of International Business Studies, 43*(1), 84–106. doi:10.1057/jibs.2011.45

Carroll, A. B. (1979). A three–dimensional conceptual model of corporate performance. *Academy of Management Review, 4*(4), 497–505. doi: 10.5465/AMR.1979.4498296

Carroll, A. B. (1991). The pyramid of corporate social responsibility: Toward the moral management of organizational stakeholders. *Business Horizons, 34*(4), 39–48. doi:10.1016/0007-6813(91)90005-G

Carroll, A. B. (1999). Corporate social responsibility: Evolution of a definitional construct. *Business & Society, 38*(3), 268–295. doi:10.1177/000765039903800303

Carroll, A. B. (2004). Managing ethically with global stakeholders: A present and future challenge. *Academy of Management Executive, 18*(2), 114–120. doi:10.5465/ame.2004.13836269

Cavusgil, S. T., Knight, G., & Riesenberger, J. R. (2012). *International business: The new realities* (2nd ed.). Upper Saddle River, NJ: Prentice Hall.

Chapple, W., & Moon, J. (2005). Corporate social responsibility (CSR) in Asia: A seven–country study of CSR web site reporting. *Business & Society, 44*(4), 415–441. doi:10.1177/0007650305281658

Chapple, W., & Moon, J. (2007). CSR agendas for Asia. *Corporate Social Responsibility and Environmental Management, 14*(4), 183–188. doi:10.1002/csr.159

Chiu, S., & Sharfman, M. P. (2011). Legitimacy, visibility, and the antecedents of corporate social performance: An investigation of instrumental perspective. *Journal of Management, 37*(6), 1558–1585. doi:10.1177/0149206309347958

Christmann, P. (2004). Multinational companies and the natural environment: Determinants of global environmental policy standardization. *Academy of Management Journal, 47*(5), 747– 760. doi:10.2307/20159616

Christmann, P., & Taylor, G. (2006). Firm self–regulation through international certifiable standards: Determinants of symbolic versus substantive implementation. *Journal of International Business Studies, 37*(6), 863–878. doi:10.1057/palgrave.jibs.8400231

Crane, A., Palazzo, G., Spence, L. J., & Matten, D. (2014). Contesting the value of "creating shared value". *California Management Review, 56*(2), 130–153. doi:10.1525/cmr.2014.56.2.130

Davis, K. (1960). Can business afford to ignore social responsibilities? *California Management Review, 2*(3), 70–76.

Delmas, M., & Toffel, M. W. (2004). Stakeholders and environmental management practices: An institutional framework. *Business Strategy and the Environment, 13*(4), 209–222. doi:10.1002/bse.409

Dögl, C., & Holtbrügge, D. (2013). Corporate environmental responsibility, employer reputation and employee commitment: An empirical study in developed and emerging economies. *The International Journal of Human Resource Management, 25*(12), 1739–1762. doi:10.1080/09585192.2013.859164

Doh, J. P., & Guay, T. R. (2006). Corporate social responsibility, public policy, and NGO activism in Europe and the United States: An institutional–stakeholder perspective. *Journal of Management Studies, 43*(1), 47–73. doi:10.1111/j.1467-6486.2006.00582.x

Doh, J., Husted, B. W., Matten, D., & Santoro, M. (2010). Ahoy there! Toward greater congruence and synergy between international business and business ethics theory and research. *Business Ethics Quarterly, 20*(3), 481–502.

Donaldson, T., & Dunfee, T. W. (1999). When ethics travel: The promise and peril of global business ethics. *California Management Review, 41*(4), 45–63. doi:10.2307/41166009

Donaldson, T., & Preston, L. E. (1995). The stakeholder theory of the corporation: Concepts, evidence, and implications. *Academy of Management Review, 20*(1), 65–91. doi:10.5465/amr.1995.9503271992

Egri, C. P., & Ralston, D. A. (2008). Corporate responsibility: A review of international management research from 1998 to 2007. *Journal of International Management, 14*(4), 319–339. doi:10.1016/j.intman.2007.09.003

Fisher, J., & Bonn, I. (2007). International strategies and ethics. *Management Decision, 45*(10), 1560–1572. doi:10.1108/00251740710837960

Font, X., Walmsley, A., Cogotti, S., McCombes, L., & Hausler, N. (2012). Corporate social responsibility: The disclosure–performance gap. *Tourism Management, 33*(6), 1544–1553. doi:10.1016/j.tourman.2012.02.012

Fortanier, F., Kolk, A., & Pinkse, J. (2011). Harmonization in CSR reporting. *Management International Review, 51*(5), 665–696. doi:10.1007/s11575-011-0089-9

Freeman, I., & Hasnaoui, A. (2011). The meaning of corporate social responsibility: The vision of four nations. *Journal of Business Ethics, 100*(3), 419–443. doi:10.1007/s10551-010-0688-6

Freeman, R. E. (1984). *Strategic management: A stakeholder approach.* Boston, MA: Pitman.

Freemann, R. E., & Reed, D. L. (1983). Stockholders and stakeholders: A new perspective on corporate governance. *California Management Review, 25*(3), 88–106.

Friedman, M. (1970, September 13). The social responsibility of business is to increase its profits. *The New York Times Magazine.* Retrieved from http://www.colorado.edu/studentgroups/libertarians/issues/friedman–soc–resp–business.html

Frooman, J. (1999). Stakeholder influence strategies. *The Academy of Management Review, 24*(2), 191–205. doi:10.5465/amr.1999.1893928

Galbreath, J. (2006). Corporate social responsibility strategy: Strategic options, global considerations. *Corporate Governance: The international journal of business in society, 6*(2), 175–187. doi:10.1108/14720700610655178

Galbreath, J. (2009). Building corporate social responsibility into strategy. *European Business Review, 21*(2), 109–127. doi:10.1108/09555340910940123

Garriga, E., & Melé, D. (2004). Corporate social responsibility theories: Mapping the territory. *Journal of Business Ethics, 53*(1–2), 51–71. doi:10.1023/B:BUSI.0000039399.90587.34

Giuliani, E., & Macchi, C. (2014). Multinational corporations economic and human rights impacts on developing countries: A review and research agenda. *Cambridge Journal of Economics, 38*(2), 479–517. doi:10.1093/cje/bet060

Hah, K., & Freeman, S. (2014). Multinational enterprise subsidiaries and their CSR: A conceptual framework of the management of CSR in smaller emerging economies. *Journal of Business Ethics, 122*(1), 125–136. doi:10.1007/s10551-013-1753-8

Hamprecht, J., & Schwarzkopf, J. (2014). Subsidiary initiatives in the institutional environment. *Management International Review, 54*(5), 757–778. doi:10.1007/s11575-014-0203-x

Harwood, I., & Humby, S. (2008). Embedding corporate responsibility into supply: A snapshot of progress. *European Management Journal, 26*(3), 166–174. doi:10.1016/j.emj.2008.01.005

Harzing, A.–W. (2000). An empirical analysis and extension of the bartlett and ghoshal typology of multinational companies. *Journal of International Business Studies, 31*(1), 101–120. doi:10.1057/palgrave.jibs.8490891

Hillman, A. J., & Wan, W. P. (2005). The determinants of MNE subsidiaries' political strategies: Evidence of institutional duality. *Journal of International Business Studies, 36*(3), 322–340. doi:10.1057/palgrave.jibs.8400137

Hsueh, C. F. (2014). Improving corporate social responsibility in a supply chain through a new revenue sharing contract. *International Journal of Production Economics, 151*(C), 214–222. doi:10.1016/j.ijpe.2013.10.017

Husted, B. W. (2005). Risk management, real options, and corporate social responsibility. *Journal of Business Ethics, 60*(2), 175–183. doi:10.1007/s10551-005-3777-1

Husted, B. W., & Allen, D. B. (2006). Corporate social responsibility in the multinational enterprise: Strategic and institutional approaches. *Journal of International Business Studies, 37*(6), 838–849. doi:10.1057/palgrave.jibs.8400227

Husted, B. W., & Allen, D. B. (2007). Corporate social strategy in multinational enterprises: Antecedents and value creation. *Journal of Business Ethics, 74*(4), 345–361. doi:10.1007/s10551-007-9511-4

Husted, B. W., Allen, D. B., & Rivera, J. E. (2010). Governance choice for strategic corporate social responsibility: Evidence from central america. *Business Society, 49*(2), 201–215. doi:10.1177/0007650308315504

Inkpen, A., & Ramaswamy, K. (2006). *Global strategy: Creating and sustaining advantage across borders.* New York, NY: Oxford University Press, Inc.

Jain, R., & De Moya, M. (2013). Global, local, or glocal: Investigating CSR strategies of best corporate citizens in India. *International Journal of Strategic Communication, 7*(3), 207–226. doi:10.1080/1553118x.2013.782548

Jamali, D. (2008). A stakeholder approach to corporate social responsibility: A fresh perspective into theory and practice. *Journal of Business Ethics, 82*(1), 213–231. doi:10.1007/s10551-007-9572-4

Jamali, D. (2010). The CSR of MNC subsidiaries in developing countries: Global, local, substantive or diluted? *Journal of Business Ethics, 93*(2), 181–200. doi:10.1007/s10551-010-0560-8

Johanson, J., & Vahlne, J.–E. (1977). The internationalization process of the firm – a model of knowledge development and increasing foreign market commitments. *Journal of International Business Studies, 8*(1), 23–32. doi:10.1057/palgrave.jibs.8490676

Jones, T. M. (1995). Instrumental stakeholder theory: A synthesis of ethics and economics. *Academy of Management Review, 20*(2), 404–437. doi:10.5465/amr.1995.9507312924

Kanji, G. K., & Chopra, P. K. (2010). Corporate social responsibility in a global economy. *Total Quality Management & Business Excellence, 21*(2), 119–143. doi:10.1080/14783360903549808

Kolk, A., & Van Tulder, R. (2004). Ethics in international business: multinational approaches to child labor. *Journal of World Business, 39*(1), 49–60. doi:10.1016/j.jwb.2003.08.014

Kolk, A., & van Tulder, R. (2010). International business, corporate social responsibility and sustainable development. *International Business Review, 19*(2), 119–125. doi:10.1016/j.ibusrev.2009.12.003

Kostova, T., & Roth, K. (2002). Adoption of an organizational practice by subsidiaries of multinational corporations: Institutional and relational effects. *Academy of Management Journal, 45*(1), 215–233. doi:10.2307/3069293

Kostova, T., & Zaheer, S. (1999). Organizational legitimacy under conditions of complexity: The case of the multinational enterprise. *Academy of Management Review, 24*(1), 64–81. doi:10.5465/amr.1999.1580441

Lai Cheng, W., & Ahmad, J. (2010). Incorporating stakeholder approach in corporate social responsibility (CSR): A case study at multinational corporations (MNCs) in Penang. *Social Responsibility Journal, 6*(4), 593–610. doi:10.1108/17471111011083464

Laudal, T. (2010). An attempt to determine the CSR potential of the international clothing business. *Journal of Business Ethics, 96*(1), 63–77. doi:10.1007/s10551-010-0449-6

Laudal, T. (2011). Drivers and barriers of CSR and the size and internationalization of firms. *Social Responsibility Journal, 7*(2), 234–256. doi:10.1108/17471111111141512

Lee, K., Oh, W.–J., & Kim, N. (2013). Social media for socially responsible firms: Analysis of fortune 500's twitter profiles and their CSR/CSIR ratings. *Journal of Business Ethics, 118*(4), 791–806. doi:10.1007/s10551-013-1961-2

Lindgreen, A., Swaen, V., & Maon, F. (2009). Introduction: Corporate social responsibility implementation. *Journal of Business Ethics, 85*(SUPPL. 2), 251–256. doi:10.1007/s10551-008-9732-1

Lo, C. W. H., Egri, C. P., & Ralston, D. A. (2008). Commitment to corporate, social, and environmental responsibilities: An insight into contrasting perspectives in China and the US. *Organization Management Journal, 5*(2), 83–98. doi:10.1057/omj.2008.10

Logsdon, J. M., & Wood, D. J. (2002). Business citizenship: From domestic to global level of analysis. *Business Ethics Quarterly, 12*(2), 155. doi:10.2307/3857809

Logsdon, J. M., & Wood, D. J. (2005). Global business citizenship and voluntary codes of ethical conduct. *Journal of Business Ethics, 59*(1–2), 55–67. doi:10.1007/s10551-005-3411-2

London, T., & Hart, S. L. (2004). Reinventing strategies for emerging markets: Beyond the transnational model. *Journal of International Business Studies, 35*(5), 350–370. doi:10.1057/palgrave.jibs.8400099

Lu, W., Chau, K. W., Wang, H., & Pan, W. (2014). A decade's debate on the nexus between corporate social and corporate financial performance: A critical review of empirical studies 2002–2011. *Journal of Cleaner Production, 79*, 195–206. doi:10.1016/j.jclepro.2014.04.072

Luo, Y. (2006). Political behavior, social responsibility, and perceived corruption: a structuration perspective. *Journal of International Business Studies, 37*(6), 747–766. doi:10.1057/palgrave.jibs.8400224

Margolis, J. D., & Walsh, J. P. (2003). Misery loves companies: Rethinking social initiatives by business. *Administrative Science Quarterly, 48*(2), 268. doi:10.2307/3556659

Matten, D., & Moon, J. (2008). "Implicit" and "explicit" CSR: A conceptual framework for a comparative understanding of corporate social responsibility. *Academy of Management Review, 33*(2), 404–424. doi:10.5465/amr.2008.31193458

McWilliams, A., & Siegel, D. (2001). Corporate social responsibility: A theory of the firm perspective. *The Academy of Management Review, 26*(1), 117–127. doi:10.5465/AMR.2001.4011987

McWilliams, A., Siegel, D. S., & Wright, P. M. (2006). Corporate social responsibility: Strategic implications. *Journal of Management Studies, 43*(1), 1–18. doi:10.1111/j.1467-6486.2006.00580.x

Meyer, K. E. (2004). Perspectives on multinational enterprises in emerging economies. *Journal of International Business Studies, 35*(4), 259–276. doi:10.1057/palgrave.jibs.8400084

Miska, C., Hilbe, C., & Mayer, S. (2014). Reconciling different views on responsible leadership: A rationality–based approach. *Journal of Business Ethics, 125*(2), 349–360. doi:10.1007/s10551-013-1923-8

Morschett, D., Schramm–Klein, H., & Zentes, J. (2009). *Strategic international management: Text and cases* (1st ed.). Wiesbaden, Germany: Gabler.

Muller, A. (2006). Global versus local CSR strategies. *European Management Journal, 24*(2–3), 189–198. doi:10.1016/j.emj.2006.03.008

Muller, A., & Kolk, A. (2009). CSR performance in emerging markets evidence from Mexico. *Journal of Business Ethics, 85*(2), 325–337. doi:10.1007/s10551–008-9735-y

Nason, R. W. (2008). Structuring the global marketplace: The impact of the united nations global compact. *Journal of Macromarketing, 28*(4), 418–425. doi:10.1177/0276146708325388

Nasrullah, N. M., & Rahim, M. M. (2014). *CSR in private enterprises in developing countries: Evidences from the ready–made garments industry in Bangladesh.* Cham, Switzerland: Springer. doi:10.1007/978-3-319-02350-2

Orlitzky, M., Schmidt, F. L., & Rynes, S. L. (2003). Corporate social and financial performance: A meta–analysis. *Organization Studies, 24*(3), 403–441. doi:10.1177/0170840603024003910

Oikonomou, I., Brooks, C., & Pavelin, S. (2014). The financial effects of uniform and mixed corporate social performance. *Journal of Management Studies, 51*(6), 898–925. doi:10.1111/joms.12064

Palazzo, G. S., & Scherer, A. G. (2006). Corporate legitimacy as deliberation: A communicative framework. *Journal of Business Ethics*, *66*(1), 71–88. doi:10.1007/s10551-006-9044-2

Park, B. I., & Ghauri, P. N. (2015). Determinants influencing CSR practices in small and medium sized MNE subsidiaries: A stakeholder perspective. *Journal of World Business*, *50*(1), 192–204. doi:10.1016/j.jwb.2014.04.007

Park, B. I., Chidlow, A., & Choi, J. (2014). Corporate social responsibility: Stakeholders influence on MNEs' activities. *International Business Review*, *23*(5), 966–980. doi:10.1016/j.ibusrev.2014.02.008

Peng, M. W., & Pleggenkuhle–Miles, E. G. (2009). Current debates in global strategy. *International Journal of Management Reviews*, *11*(1), 51–68. doi:10.1111/j.1468-2370.2008.00249.x

Polonsky, M., & Jevons, C. (2009). Global branding and strategic CSR: An overview of three types of complexity. *International Marketing Review*, *26*(3), 327–347. doi:10.1108/02651330910960816

Popoli, P. (2011). Linking CSR strategy and brand image: Different approaches in local and global markets. *Marketing Theory*, *11*(4), 419–433. doi:10.1177/1470593111418795

Porter, M. E. (1996). What is Strategy? *Harvard Business Review*, *74*(6), 61–78.

Porter, M. E., & Kramer, M. R. (2002). The competitive advantage of corporate philanthropy. *Harvard Business Review*, *80*(12), 56–69.

Porter, M. E., & Kramer, M. R. (2006). Strategy & society: The link between competitive advantage and corporate social responsibility. *Harvard Business Review*, *84*(12), 78–92.

Porter, M. E., & Kramer, M. R. (2011). The big idea: Creating shared value. *Harvard Business Review*, *89*(1/2), 62–77.

Prahalad, C. K. (2012). Bottom of the pyramid as a source of breakthrough innovations. *Journal of Product Innovation Management*, *29*(1), 6–12. doi:10.1111/j.1540-5885.2011.00874.x

Prahalad, C. K., & Doz, Y. (Ed.). (1987). *The multinational mission: Balancing local demands and global vision*. New York, NY: The Free Press.

Prieto–Carrón, M., Lund–Thomsen, P., Chan, A., Muro, A., & Bhushan, C. (2006). Critical perspectives on CSR and development: What we know, what we don't know, and what we need to know. *International Affairs*, *82*(5), 977–987. doi:10.1111/j.1468-2346.2006.00581.x

Rangan, K., Chase, L., & Karim, S. (2015). The truth about CSR. *Harvard Business Review*, *93*(1/2), 40–49.

Reimann, F., Ehrgott, M., Kaufmann, L., & Carter, C. R. (2012). Local stakeholders and local legitimacy: MNEs' social strategies in emerging economies. *Journal of International Management*, *18*(1), 1–17. doi:10.1016/j.intman.2011.06.002

Robertson, D. C. (2009). Corporate social responsibility and different stages of economic development: Singapore, Turkey, and Ethiopia. *Journal of Business Ethics*, *88*(4), 617–633. doi:10.1007/s10551-009-0311-x

Rodriguez, P., Siegel, D. S., Hillman, A. & Eden, L. (2006). Three lenses on the multinational enterprise: Politics, corruption, and corporate social responsibility. *Journal of International Business Studies, 37*(6), 733–746. doi:10.1057/palgrave.jibs.8400229

Russo, M. V., & Fouts, P. A. (1997). A resource–based perspective on corporate environmental performance and profitability. *Academy of Management Journal, 40*(3), 534–559. doi:10.2307/257052

Salomon, R., & Wu, Z. (2012). Institutional distance and local isomorphism strategy. *Journal of International Business Studies, 43*(4), 343–367. doi:10.1057/jibs.2012.3

Saunders, M., Lewis, P., & Thornhill, A. (2009). Research methods for business students (5th ed.). Harlow, England: Prentice Hall.

Scherer, A. G., & Palazzo, G. (2011). The new political role of business in a globalized world: A review of a new perspective on CSR and its implications for the firm, governance, and democracy. *Journal of Management Studies, 48*(4), 899–931. doi:10.1111/j.1467-6486.2010.00950.x

Schneider, A. (2014). Embracing ambiguity – lessons from the study of corporate social responsibility throughout the rise and decline of the modern welfare state. *Business Ethics: A European Review, 23*(3), 293–308. doi:10.1111/beer.12052

Schwartz, M. S., & Carroll, A. B. (2003). Corporate Social Responsibility. *Business Ethics Quarterly, 13*(4), 503–530. doi:10.5840/beq200313435

Sharfman, M. P., Shaft, T. M., & Tihanyi, L. (2004). A model of the global and institutional antecedents of high–level corporate environmental performance. *Business & Society, 43*(1), 6–36. doi:10.1177/0007650304262962

Simola, S. K. (2007). The pragmatics of care in sustainable global enterprise. *Journal of Business Ethics, 74*(2), 131–147. doi:10.1007/s10551-006-9225-z

Sison, A. J. G. (2009). From CSR to corporate citizenship: Anglo–American and continental European perspectives. *Journal of Business Ethics, 89*(3), 235–246. doi:10.1007/s10551-010-0395-3

Snider, J., Hill, R. P., & Martin, D. (2003). Corporate social responsibility in the 21st century: A view from the world's most successful firms. *Journal of Business Ethics, 48*(2), p.175–187. doi:10.1023/b:busi.0000004606.29523.db

Stahl, G. K., & de Luque, M. S. (2014). Antecedents of responsible leader behavior: A research synthesis, conceptual framework, and agenda for future research. *Academy of Management Perspectives, 28*(3), 235–254. doi:10.5465/amp.2013.0126

Strange, S. (1996). *The retreat of the state: The diffusion of power in the world economy.* Cambridge, England: Cambridge University Press.

Strike, V. M., Gao, J., & Bansal, P. (2006). Being good while being bad: Social responsibility and the international diversification of us firms. *Journal of International Business Studies, 37*(6), 850–862. doi:10.1057/palgrave.jibs.8400226

Sweeney, L., & Coughlan, J. (2008). Do different industries report corporate social responsibility differently? An investigation through the lens of stakeholder theory. *Journal of Marketing Communications, 14*(2), 113–124. doi:10.1080/13527260701856657

Tan, J., & Wang, L. (2011). MNC strategic responses to ethical pressure: An institutional logic perspective. *Journal of Business Ethics*, *98*(3), 373–390. doi: 10.1007/s10551-010-0553-7

UN Global Compact Office. (2014). *UN Global Compact* [Brochure]. New York, NY: United Nations. Retrieved from https://www.unglobalcompact.org/docs/news_events/8.1/GC_brochure_FINAL.pdf

Van Tulder, R., & Kolk, A. (2001). Multinationality and corporate ethics: Codes of conduct in the sporting goods industry. *Journal of International Business Studies*, *32*(2), 267–283. doi:10.1057/palgrave.jibs.8490952

Voegtlin, C., & Pless, N. M. (2014). Global governance: CSR and the role of the un global compact. *Journal of Business Ethics*, *122*(2), 179–191. doi:10.1007/s10551-014-2214-8

Waddock, S. (2008). Building a new institutional infrastructure for corporate responsibility. *Academy of Management Perspectives*, *22*(3), 87–108. doi:10.5465/amp.2008.34587997

Waldman, D. A., Sully de Luque, M., Washburn, N., House, R. J., Adetoun, B., Barrasa, A., Wilderom, C. P. M. (2006). Cultural and leadership predictors of corporate social responsibility values of top management: A GLOBE study of 15 countries. *Journal of International Business Studies*, *37*(6), 823–837. doi:10.1057/palgrave.jibs.8400230

Werther, W. B. Jr., & Chandler, D. (2006). *Strategic corporate social responsibility: Stakeholders in a global environment*. Thousand Oaks, CA: SAGE Publications.

Wiig, A., & Kolstad, I. (2010). Multinational corporations and host country institutions: A case study of CSR activities in Angola. *International Business Review*, *19*(2), 178–190. doi:10.1016/j.ibusrev.2009.11.006

Williams, C. A., & Aguilera, R. V. (2008). Corporate social responsibility in a comparative perspective. In Crane, A., et al. *The Oxford handbook of corporate social responsibility*. Oxford: Oxford University Press. doi:10.1093/oxfordhb/9780199211593.003.0020

Williams, G., & Zinkin, J. (2009). Islam and CSR: A study of the compatibility between the tenets of Islam and the UN global compact. *Journal of Business Ethics*, *91*(4), 519–533. doi:10.1007/s10551-009-0097-x

Windsor, D. (2013). Corporate social responsibility and irresponsibility: A positive theory approach. *Journal of Business Research*, *66*(10), 1937–1944. doi:10.1016/j.jbusres. '2013.02.016

Yang, X., & Rivers, C. (2009). Antecedents of CSR practices in MNCs' subsidiaries: A stakeholder and institutional perspective. *Journal of Business Ethics*, *86*(2), 155–169. doi:10.1007/s10551-009-0191-0

Young, S. L., & Makhija, M. V. (2014). Firms' corporate social responsibility behavior: An integration of institutional and profit maximization approaches. *Journal of International Business Studies*, *45*(6), 670–698. doi:10.1057/jibs.2014.29

Zhao, M. (2012). CSR–based political legitimacy strategy: Managing the state by doing good in China and Russia. *Journal of Business Ethics*, *111*(4), 439–460. doi:10.1007/s10551-012-1209-6

Zhao, M., Park, S. H., & Zhou, N. (2014). MNC strategy and social adaptation in emerging markets. *Journal of International Business Studies*, *45*(7), 842–861. doi:10.1057/jibs.2014.8